Rx: A Dose of Heart

An ER Physician's
Remarkable Stories of the
Heart's Power to Renew and
Transform Our Lives.

Gil Burgstede, M.D.

Fourth Edition
ISBN# 978-0-9830479-2-6

Dedicated to and in Memory of:

W. Brugh Joy, M.D.

With a Radiance of Love
Fellow physician, mentor and beloved teacher of
the heart center's life fulfilling energies.

A physician once said, "A dose of love is the most powerful medicine in the world."

A patient then asked, "What if that isn't enough?"

The physician smiled and replied, "Then increase the dose."

This is the story of increasing the dose a million fold, by liberating the unifying energy (also called love) fully...

Table of Contents

In Acknowledgment

I would like to acknowledge all of those who have inspired and supported my lifelong journey in the healing arts.

Thank you to all of the teachers since my childhood who told stories, in so many different forms, about those who had the wisdom, power and courage to heal and love deeply and expansively

Thank you to the teachers who guided and inspired my interest in the scientific world and in the study of human behavior, as well as my mentors in medical school and residency.

My heart-felt gratitude overflows to the entire hospital staff, especially the nurses I've worked with side by side, day and night, as we've tended to those in times of great need, for their tireless devotion, dedication, unique contributions and care. While I tended to the technical aspects of medicine, they always tended to the human.

Also my gratitude goes to Kenneth Bill, M.D., my childhood hero and the man who inspired me to become Dr. Gil. To Jerry Salan, M.D., for his passion and dedication to medicine and community, and for being a mentor to me when I started practice with him and his partners in 1979.

To Brugh Joy, M.D., for having had the courage to depart from a successful medical practice and traditional life; to begin traveling the world to study and experience ancient and multicultural philosophies and modalities of healing. Brugh introduced me to the mystery of the heart center as an energetic locus that engages the attributes of unconditional love, a healing presence, innate harmony and compassion. His conferences on the healing and transformational aspects of the heart center taught me to search inwardly for the answers to life's most challenging questions and situations. "Centering," through engaging the unifying energy of the energetic heart, became the foundation for my life's journey. My thanks also go to a woman who gave up her identity and everything she owned to become, Peace Pilgrim. For 28 years she walked over 25,000 miles across this country with one message: Inner peace brings about outer peace. Her only possessions: her clothes, a toothbrush, a comb, and the abundant radiance of her love and unconditional service to life. She inspired millions, all of whom were touched by her words, her healing presence and her stories. She was deeply connected to her heart and once said, "I am always at home where ever I am." Walking for inner peace even into her seventies, with her long white hair and radiant presence, she embodied the love of the universal heart and service to all of humanity.

Additionally, I am grateful for my wife Janis DeLuca—for the many, many nights she listened and tended to my confusing inner struggles with work (in a curing environment) and the search for healing—offering great insight, wisdom, and compassion. Her presence and commitment to the inner journey and bringing joy to life has been a constant blessing to me.

Thank you to our children, Annie and Adam, and their heart-full enlivening presence, their wonderful music, and their dreams for a better tomorrow.

Thank you to the initial readers of this text and their rich and guiding comments: Barb Achten, Kari Esbensen, Rachel Hoyer, Kathryn Jeffers, Tim Koll, Rick Munster and Nancy Thorson.

Thank you to my editor Nick Marco, whose insight and wisdom laden comments helped shape so many aspects of this book.

Thank you to Kia Hellman for the final edit and ongoing enthusiasm for this book's message.

Thank you to Casey Medema for proofreading with such care and accuracy.

Thank you to Lisa Hoffman for the striking cover design that so beautifully conveys the emergence of unifying energy from within.

Thank you life for a chance encounter with the sister and the grandmother of Shauna Lee (Chapter Five), who urged me to complete this book after it had laid neglected in the back of the closet for over a year with no intention of being published. Sometimes it takes a specific series of events to open us up to the importance of sharing with this world all that is in the center of our hearts.

And in memory of Dave Warner, M.D., Brugh Joy, M.D., Dorothy Wolfe Clayton and John Denver.

***

I am grateful for all of the healing encounters with the individuals mentioned in this text, who, in the darkest times of life, have revealed the priceless gift of healing and unifying energy that comes from the depths of the heart.

The dates of most events in this book have been omitted, and I've changed the names of several patients and colleagues to protect their identities. Likewise, in order to protect privacy, I've chosen not to reveal the locations of the hospital and emergency room encounters I've written about in the following pages.

And thank you, the reader, for being open to the process of heart centering, the unifying energy also called heart power, and this universal journey into wholeness we are being called to engage.

Disclaimer

This text introduces *heart centering* as a modern energetic process to shift from an energetically stress-full to a heart-full life and reality. Under no circumstance is centering a substitute for appropriate medical care. As always, a thorough evaluation and treatment for any emotional, physical, psychological, or mental conditions of concern, by a competent healthcare professional, is advised.

Introduction

Rx: A Dose of Heart

Outer successfulness always leads to inner emptiness.
Our apocalyptic crisis of separation from the heart intensifies.

In the midst of a reality of virtual screens of light, intense polarization and dark times where do we look now for the guiding light to liberate us?

Our first encounter with the power of centering and energetic unity happened as newborns, in our mother's arms. There, in her embrace, we were deeply connected heart to heart as both of us were mutually filled with infusions of unifying energy. Once filled we then separated from that event to continue on our mentally focused outer journey to successfully become separate Supermen and Superwomen with our strong armor/ego identity, this left us increasingly separated from the heart and "heart energy depleted." But before that phase of our journey ended **a second outer encounter with the power of the heart center and its unifying energy was needed**. It was an unconscious embrace that made our chest ache and feel warm and transformed our world and our reality into one of beauty and fulfillment; it was labeled romantic love. Little did we understand how that reconnection to the heart and experience of unity between two opposites shifted us into the three-dimensional reality of the heart. But it filled us enough so we could continue the phase of development called being outwardly successful and separate.

This phase resulted in **further separation from our hearts**. With the departure of "love," **we were left halfhearted or half whole**, and remained intellectually naïve in our capacity to understand what happened or how to experience "healing/love" like that again. We returned to our outer work of intellectually (mind power) and physically (body power) continuing our outer journey. We've achieved successfulness in creating a strong and

11

thickly armored separate surface self that was mentally powerful, yet powerless to change. **Super-selves, limited to outer interactions and stabilizing lives** on the surface level but left with a confusing, insatiable hunger and yearning under our armor. The **answers were always out there** and so the outer search continues and intensifies, but increasingly we find this stage of our development disappointing us as the sense of "something profound is missing" increases every day. Attempts to externally resolve this unrealized, unconscious "inner emptiness" leaves us outwardly stressed out, burned out, zoned out and needing addictions to cope, as well as experiencing increased polarization and separation in our relationships. Then struggling, stuck and silently suffering in the mind's reality, **the apocalyptic breaking point appears, where we begin breaking down.**

An intellectual understanding of this crisis of change and attempts to apply the "curing paradigm" of fixing and controlling individual "symptoms" and stabilizing outer lives is no longer enough. **But, through understanding our many "symptoms" as having a singular cause,** the correct diagnosis (Dx:) becomes clear:

Mind: Stressed **out**, too much energy to the mind (overloaded).

Heart: Zoned **out**, blocked from accessing the heart's energy.

Body: Burned **out**, energy depleted, neglected.

A 100% **outwardly** focused surface-oriented two-dimensional reality and separation energies! Angry and polarized men stuck holding on to old roles and mind power. Angry and polarized women stuck holding on to body power. In this reality, both are profoundly disconnected from the heart. And like everyone else addicted to virtual lights that give no answers. A time and reality that has become false and fake in its capacity to satisfy our deepest needs and desires. A time and reality of darkness with no true guiding light!

And now we are in the "emergency room" of life, facing a life-threatening condition. **The correct diagnosis is inner emptiness due to disconnection from the heart!** Living but dead, shells without any "unifying" heart energy left. **No love left** for ourselves or others. Living countless repetitive days looking outside of ourselves, and unable to change our reality.

With the correct "energetic diagnosis" we can use the correct energetic prescription of *Heart Centering* for reconnecting to our hearts and giving and receiving "Doses of Unifying Energy." With centering, we can begin the process of energetically infusing and nourishing ourselves and each other (over and over again) with doses of Life's Most Powerful Medicine, which is underline unifying energy, to become heart-full and then soul-full (whole)!

Breaking Free of the Crisis!

Together, the stories of this text are a living reflection of challenges faced while transforming our lives by reconnecting to the unifying effect of being heart centered. These stories are filled with remarkable people in the ER who "find their center" in the midst of intense energetic life crises, addictions, suicide attempts, and even death, and emerge to experience, in those moments, the heart's reality of fullness and radiance.

As transforming as my earliest experiences were with *Heart Centering*, my deepest understanding came in the form of a teenage boy, who demanded the answer to his personal crisis, or he would kill himself. The strange death that transpired confirmed that in our greatest storms, **we are destined to come together** and center to reconnect to our hearts and find the calm (inner peace) of the heart's power and reality.

When the Belief in Love's Return Becomes Reality

Consciously centering to reconnect to our hearts, the heart's reality returns as an internalized unifying event, experienced as deep and expansive love of self and others. From energetic emptiness within to heart-fullness and wholeness (a radiance of love).

The Science of "Energy and Love"
Becoming Energy Savvy.

Its all about learning how to shift from the information age and our old mental reality of separation, to the energy age with unifying energies and the new heart-centered reality

of unity. It's changing the focus of our awareness from virtual and manipulated light to the real light of the heart. *Using the Universal Law of Reality.* Engaging Life Like an Einstein. **It's All About Energy and Energy Medicine! From E=mc² (everything is energy in one form or another) To E+F=R (Energy + Focus = Reality.** Energy always flows to where we focus our awareness and creates our reality) Before each life changing event in the ER, **a simple yet profound process** was used to shift and energetically experience **"Being Balanced, Unified, Empowered and Fulfilled from Within."** This modern, energetically based process is called **Heart Centering.*** With Heart Centering, we can reconnect to our hearts and shift out of the separation energies and emptiness created by the Information Age and overcome our fear of a reality change.

Center Yourself and Enter Einstein's Energy Age to know that:
Energy + Focus = Reality

If we focus outwardly on the surface of things, nothing changes. We remain internally empty and limited to living in the mind's old two-dimensional reality with separating and polarizing energies.

If we reconnect to our hearts by focusing on the center within, we can fill ourselves with unifying energy and radiate that energy outwardly. Everything transforms as we experience the heart's reality of unity. From the virtual (and empty) life of zombies to the real life of transformers.

The PBC's of Centering for Healing, Health and Wholeness.
Pause and stop looking outwardly and energizing the same old superficial mental programs, beliefs, and behaviors that keep you stuck in a surface reality and separated from your heart, and instead focus inwardly.
Breathe to release all bound tension from your armored body.
Center to empower a calm, integrated (unified) self.
Share the overflow of unifying energy with others.

The stories in this book will reveal your capacity and destiny to center and reconnect to your heart. They will also show you how to penetrate your armor and any layers of anger, fear, hope, need, greed, envy, jealousy, abandonment, self-fear, self-judgment, self-punishment, self-righteousness, self-pity, self-doubt, self-denial, self-destruction, self-blame, and self-betrayal. The stories will help you break free to love and nourish your life, deeply and expansively.

Its time to go beyond our old identities as weary supermen and superwomen who are disconnected from our hearts and becoming heartless zombies. It's time to embrace our new identities as energy savvy, passionate, heart-centered champions, and wise soulful elders.

Its time to experience our heart's natural attributes of unconditional love, a healing presence, innate harmony, compassion, and service to life.

And now we begin the amazing journey to reconnect to our heart centers, moving beyond virtual reality addiction and its incapacity to fulfill us, to renewing, fulfilling and transforming ourselves through sharing the unifying energy called love as never before possible. Centering over and over again to go from profound inner emptiness to heart-fullness and wholeness **as together we begin** the heart centering revolution for all…

*Please note that all references to the heart, heart center, heart centering and centering in this text refer to our symbolic, geometric, anatomical, psychological, emotional and *energetic* center which happens to lie within the area of the physical heart.

Part I

Searching

Something profound is missing in our lives.

The confusing yet profoundly beautiful and courageous search begins—to end our inner emptiness and overcome our fear of change, as we shift from the two-dimensional reality of the mind and body and the manipulated reality of our screens, to the three-dimensional reality of the heart. Overcoming the confusion, emptiness and fear of the information age—to enter the energy age and experience wisdom, heartfulness and the courage to change through fully liberating unifying energy (love) from within.

1
The Power of Centering

It's the great dream of humanity.
That in the darkest of times the heart would be found again and
its full power radiantly liberated for all.

"He said he's going to kill himself today, unless you have the answer."
His silent suffering was so great.
He wanted to die... like so many others.

Knowing I wished to see such patients, the nurse said, "This chart's for you," and she handed me the clipboard.

She shook her head from side to side in dismay.

"He said he's going to kill himself today, unless you have the answer."

Jake's demand was the greatest life had ever presented to me. The pain and suffering of his everyday mental reality had brought him to the breaking point. What unfolded in that next hour revealed the most important discovery of my medical career and life.

His suffering and request was so profound it became the beginning statement of this book and his transformative death so radiant and life fulfilling it became the last story, as an endless chapter in the quest to love life deeply and expansively.

This book is filled with stories like his, of so many becoming casualties of the information age, because of unrealized separation from the heart. Yet, it also speaks of the greatest of human capacities, of becoming energy savvy and reconnecting to our hearts in a new and glorious way, to love and heal as never before possible.

It begins as a past testament to the greatest of stories, your own story: of physical birth and physical survival, of mental programming to fit in with learned patterns of behavior, beliefs and roles, of glorious love found and lost, of successfulness and its unrealized inner emptiness, of being mentally stressed out, physically burned out and heart fully zoned out, of needing addictions to cope, of polarization in your outer relationships, of being manipulated by virtual reality screens, of an apocalyptic breaking point and now of the greatest gift you can give and receive.

Letting go of old ways and roles and centering and opening your hands as a new empowered heart centered self. To stand in the midst of the winds of change and liberate your heart's full radiant power of unifying energy, to renew, fulfill and transform your life, over and over again; a true liberation of love and life.

We begin with the great story of physical birth.

2

Paradise Lost

As a child we held a great dream.
No child and no dream should die.

Our first home and the first stage of our lives began inside her.

Breath after breath after breath, gently rocking our body in the dark warmth of her womb.

Lub, dub, lub, dub, lub, dub the endless heartbeat of our mother and the energy of unity it carried—and the physical nourishment its blood carried—to create an exquisite new body. Sheltered and protected until the day when there was no more room and change had to happen, it was destiny. Suddenly a *physical crisis* struck.

***

"The heart rate is dropping," the nurse said.

Babies weren't supposed to die so close to delivery. They just weren't.

This isn't right. This isn't the way it's supposed to be. Babies aren't supposed to die, I thought to myself.

It was something I dreaded more than anything else—the death of a baby. The death of a baby and all the unrealized dreams of joy and love it held.

Anna and her baby were in the third stage of physical labor, the most intense stage, and the breaking point was near.

I looked at her again. Beads of sweat forming on her forehead, ready for the next contraction. Gathering her strength again, arms tightening their grip on the railings of the bed.

It had been a long night since her labor began, and fatigue was settling in. After nine months of absolute calm, physical forces suddenly and unexpectedly struck, nearly overwhelming her—especially since this was her first baby. She had a tight birth canal, and it was an intense labor. For the unprepared or unsupported, it can be especially painful and overwhelming during the latter hours of the process.

However, like so many women in my obstetrical practice, she and her husband had been well trained in Lamaze, which is an amazing breath-centered tool and process that had not always been available. Before Lamaze was introduced, in my experiences as a resident, deliveries were difficult—filled with screams of pain and fear—and needed potent painkillers. With Lamaze, women empowered themselves while in physical labor. They modified their reaction to intense discomfort and were not overwhelmed by the physical stress that the labor process can create. They were breathing through the stress of physical pain, using the mind and body's innate capacities to move through the pain of physical labor, creating and connecting to a calm breath while centering their awareness on a focal point like a target on the wall. Creating calm in the midst of physical storm—how novel! How wonderful! How empowering to witness labor now!

At our hospital, an excellent OB staff taught the technique. In fact, Pat, her nurse in attendance, had also been her Lamaze instructor. As an experienced guide and mentor, Pat was able to reassure through her presence alone. With the baby's father and another nurse, we made a team of five, and we all understood the dynamics of this natural transition for the baby and the mother.

We were well trained and we were there for each other—all physically there and energetically supporting each other through the early morning hours. The cervix, which is the opening between the womb and the pelvic passageway, had been opening slowly and continuously. Although it had been long, the labor of transition for the infant had unfolded naturally. Anna's innate strength, skills, and capacities were profoundly beautiful and empowering to witness. She was the vehicle of a miracle.

But a crisis was evolving as the baby's head did not come down as quickly as expected; the passageway was tighter than usual and the pain increasingly intense.

Anna continued. Breathing slowing, going inwardly, focusing inwardly, inwardly and downwardly. Pushing with her head and neck down and then neck arching back. Sweat streaming off her forehead. Ahhh, ahhh, ahhh…, then silence and rapid breathing. Eyes remaining closed, recovering breath and focus.

"The heart rate is dropping again," Pat said, trying to remain as calm as possible. It was a crisis I had been trained to deal with. After all of the deliveries I had experienced with my mentors in residency, the hundreds and hundreds of babies I had delivered since, the long hours of waiting for the birth and preparing to do the best I could—after all of that experience and preparation, it came down to trust—deep trust in my present actions and those to come.

Glancing over at the monitor, I saw the heart rate being traced on the red grid of a white paper strip four inches wide. The monitor was pouring out a paper confirmation: danger, danger, danger! After each contraction, the baby's heart rate was dropping. It had gone from the 140s, which was normal, to the 80s and then 70s, where it had stayed for a far longer time than expected. I had many thoughts:

Things are really going bad here!

Maybe the umbilical cord is wrapped around the baby's neck, strangulating it. Maybe the baby is infected and the stress of labor is too much.

Though extremely rare, the cord sometimes wraps around the neck two or three times. Then, as the baby comes down, the cord begins to tighten and tighten and tighten like a noose, since it is still attached to the placenta behind it. Finally, it becomes so tight that the blood traveling through the cord is stopped and the baby gets no oxygen. In only four to five minutes without oxygen, even if the heart is pumping, the baby can experience brain injury and even brain death.

Everything will be fine. Everything will be fine.

"Everything is going to be fine," I said aloud. It was my job to be in control, to know what to do, to have the answers to every situation and crisis. But inside my green gown, my body was getting hot, very hot. Tiny droplets were flowing down the sides of my chest, and sweat was emerging from my forehead too.

Keep your fears hidden. Don't let them leak out, others will feel them. Stay calm and stay in control.

It was time for life's first dream of love to reveal itself, time for the baby to come out into the world and continue to feel the love of its mother's heart.

Dreams should not die.

This isn't going right. The baby's head is still way too high.

I looked at Pat. She knew we were crashing.

We'll need to use forceps. A C-section can't be done. There won't be time.

"Everything is going to be fine," I repeated. "We are just going to have to get the baby out faster than we thought. We'll have to use forceps."

My inner tension was increasing. My eyes peered out between mask and cap, silently communicating the depth of the crisis to the nurse.

"Get Dr. Jerry," I said calmly to the other nurse. She stepped out of the room.

We could lose this one. It's getting worse.

"Bring me the Laffee forceps."

Way too high, Gil, way too high. This will be too dangerous. It won't work. The baby will be injured even if it's possible to get it out.

Quickly I reached for medication to help numb up the pelvic passage. I slid my left hand into the pelvis along the left side of this sacred life-birthing passage, then slipped a thin metal guide carrying a needle inside, along my index finger, to just the right spot. There I delivered a small amount of medication to numb the passageway. I repeated the process on the right side.

The forceps arrived. They were my special forceps, and as they were brought into the room, they came in with the wisdom and resources of my obstetrical mentor, Dr. Bernstein, who had taught me how to use them. They were his special forceps. Unwrapping them from the sterile protective cloth, I felt them infusing me with confidence. Touching the forceps, my hands and his became one—all of his wisdom, which had been passed down through the centuries and into modern obstetrics, was within me. These forceps, unlike others, were shorter and spoon-like, and the locking mechanism was at the end rather than in the middle. They were unique in that they did not have the pliers-like effect of other forceps, but worked like two hands holding either side of the baby's head.

Move quickly now; the heart rate is staying down.

I could see the nurses preparing for a "bad" baby.

I slipped the right forceps in and then the left. I locked them at the end where I would grab hold. I pulled.

We're too high up! Never ever had to pull this hard before. This isn't going to work. We're going to lose this one.

I pulled again.

"Anna, you're going to have to push harder. We've got to get this baby out, now!"

Nothing. Rock-hard stuck. This can't be happening.

And yet it was happening. It was so close. So close, and yet the worst was happening.

Thoughts of the disaster were creeping in. The tissue in the lower part of the pelvis was not yet stretched, and the head, while being pushed through an already tight pelvis, had become stuck just before getting halfway. I knew that a head this high was a very difficult delivery with forceps, and not to be done except under the most dire circumstances. The baby could die right there in the passageway. After nine months of preparing for this one life-changing moment, it could remain stuck and die, unable to transition. And there was nothing the baby or Anna or I could do.

Dead baby.
Dead baby.
Get ready for a dead baby.
Heart rate staying down now, staying down.

At that moment, Dr. Jerry arrived. With fifteen more years of experience, he had been my mentor, introducing me to the ways of the country doctor. As our eyes locked, the strength to try one more time infused through me.

"Anna, push as hard as you can," I said as the next contraction began.

The nurses supported Anna on one side and began pushing down on her abdomen, while I began pulling on the other side.

Her neck flexed again, chin to chest. Her teeth clenched. Chest and abdominal muscles tensed like steel. And all the bodies in the room became tense; all the forces of humanity were pushing, pressing and directing forces downward. All the forces were coming together into a birthing symphony of strength and determination. Mind, body and heart strained together, yearned together.

Alleluia! We were giving everything that could be given. Everything. Alleluia! Our minds, bodies and hearts strained with her. We were all energized together. Alleluia!

I pulled harder, but nothing was moving. Nothing was happening. We were stuck.

The baby was stuck in the birth canal, unable to break through.

We have to break free. We have to break free now!

Jerry's left hand came down over both of mine. It rested on top, and then gripped down. We pulled with increasing force. It was only a little bit more, but just enough. The door between the garden of the womb and the outer world began to open. The child who carried so many dreams was being birthed that day.

Breaking free now. Breaking free!
Critical moment now.
Breaking free.

"Ahhh!..." Anna's scream of painful joy filled the room.

Releasing her breath, releasing the tension held so long.

The baby's head breaking free, emerging from the darkness, moving toward the intense lights and sounds of a new life.

An incision called an episiotomy was quickly made on the outside of the pelvic passage, and the last bit of thick tissue that held the baby back was released.

A head with dark hair crowned further, quickly stretching the remaining outer tissues of the pelvic passage. It emerged, bluish and limp. Quickly, the baby's mouth was suctioned out.

Yes, it was the cord!

The cord, wrapped tightly three times around the neck, was quickly clamped, cut, and released. The physical connection to the world of the womb, through which the crimson waters flowed with nourishment, was severed forever. Moving swiftly with a slight downward pressure, I released the upper shoulder, and then the rest of the body rapidly glided out into the new world of bright lights and sounds that were there to awaken his mind to new experiences. But the baby's body was limp and lifeless. His head fell backward, hanging loosely at the neck, like a ball at the end of a rope.

A lifeless baby, a blue baby.

Jerry grabbed the baby, taking it to the resuscitation table nearby. Floppy, no breath. Gently, he slapped the baby's soles: slap, slap, slap. He shook the baby gently side to side, then slapped the soles again: slap, slap, slap.

We turned the oxygen on also, administering breaths of oxygen from the resuscitation bag. Breaths of life to keep the baby alive, a baby that couldn't breathe on its own.

Are we too late for this baby?

Fifteen seconds went by, and nothing happened.

After thirty seconds, the baby was still blue, but a heart rate was present, up to 80.

Forty-five seconds passed, and then a slight movement.

After sixty seconds, it took the first faint breath.

And soon, the first cry!

Laughter broke out. In the midst of chaos, in the midst of storm, a miracle had occurred: birth.

Anna's face was filling with joyful tears, as I smiled under my mask.

In that moment, in all her magnificence, she was the feminine body of all women. And the child, the gift she had carried for all of humanity, had arrived with all of its dreams and potentials held inside.

As Dr. Jerry and the nurses tended to the baby, I waited as the placenta released itself.

Shortly, Anna received her child. Her hands reaching out and then bringing her new born to the center of her chest, right over her waiting heart. From physical separation to heart-filling union. The crying stopped, her arms gently and completely enfolded her son. Her eyes in awe then needing to close, feeling the grace, the beauty and the love more deeply. Her heart beating, comforting and connecting heart to heart. The heart comforting both, the heartbeat and the heart's energy. Little heart and big heart communicating, energetically networking, nurturing and supporting. Gentle rocking beginning, child resting in the natural peace of the heart again.

Leaving the world and reality of the body.
Her heart held next to his heart. Heart to heart.
The unseen center between them ignited and igniting
And the garden of life was full and whole again.
The world and reality of the mind yet to come.

Often, after labor, in the special moments between mothers and their newborn children, there were tears. Some tears would come because of the death of that special connection they had had, of infant within mother and the instinctual and innate love that flowed through her body to the infant body. The temple of the womb, once so full, filled to capacity, was now empty. The separation and emptiness was so intense for some mothers, that it created a deep depression.

Some tears would come because of the sheer beauty of the birth experience and the appearance of the child seemingly out of nothingness.

Some tears would come because of the mother's awareness of the suffering and difficult times the child would have to face in the future, difficulties a mother's nurturing love cannot protect against.

Some mothers began to worry immediately for their baby—as if they dreaded the future—a time when a mother's worst fears could become reality.

Please let this child be the one to know something different!

For thousands of years, mothers have hoped and yearned for a time when this miracle would happen to their child—something different, a different world, a different reality for their child.

For my child, let it be different.

For my child, let it be different.

For my child, let it be different.

Millions and millions and millions of times, this silent prayer was said.

For thousands and thousands of years this deepest of petitions was sent from the hearts of all mothers who are still...

Waiting, waiting, always waiting—for the fulfillment of this prayer and petition for their children and for all children.

Yet for each child born in modern times, the deep physical connection with the mother would ironically be shorter and the separation from the mother's body and disconnection from her heart and its unifying energy would occur sooner, as the mental intensities and demands of modern living increased.

A bonding experience once lasting years, to create an emotionally balanced human being was radically changed, the bottom line now demanded a mere twelve, anxious weeks. Society was no longer recognizing the value of nurturing human beings, in its rush to discipline and educate in the mind's two-dimensional reality and increasingly engage virtual realities. What would happen to these children and their capacity to love and nurture later in life?

3

The Pursuit of Happiness

*What happens when the phase of mentally pursuing happiness
and outer success comes to a completion?*

The story of the second stage of life begins with the
programming of our minds, to create our armor and defend our
beliefs of who and what we are as supermen and superwomen
living in a two-dimensional mentally created and controlled
reality. Called first by the mind to fit in and successfully live
separate, outwardly focused lives in the reality of the mind. My
search for happiness (more success) during this stage was no
different than any other.

I was born in Amsterdam, The Netherlands. I immigrated
with my parents to America, leaving behind the scars of World
War II in the hopes of experiencing the dreams of a new life.
Lady Liberty welcomed us in New York harbor.

Gloriously, like a dream, she rose out of the deepest waters in
a flowing green gown, her hand stretching upward, holding her
light high, shining for all the world to see. That light held the
promise of a new beginning, the freedom to *pursue happiness,* to
achieve your highest potential and to be the best you possibly
could—to be outwardly successful.

We settled in southeastern Wisconsin, living with an aunt on
a small dairy farm. Life for me was filled with running in the
forests and fields of paradise and playing until dusk.

But suddenly life changed, as I sat rigidly in the school desks
of our parochial school, listening to stories of the life journey.
First of the garden of paradise—a place without judgment or
punishment or rewards or fear or hope. Of a garden holding two
additional future potentials represented in two trees: a life of
struggle in a world of separation of mind from body or the
potential for a life experience of wholeness. It revealed the loss
of the one-dimensional reality of the maternal garden and the
beginning of the mentally created, mentally controlled and
mentally stabilized two-dimensional reality of the paternal mind.

This shift was presented as a story of eating of the fruit and thus seeds of the tree of good and evil. The mind's development then become more important and the creation of a new two-dimensional bipolar surface reality of the mind occurred for humanity and the desert years began. Men took over and **his**tory of stories of male leaders and followers ensued, of mental discipline as the conditional love of the father then ruled as the instinctual love of the mother for the body was released. **Her**story of nurturing and the garden ended. Nurturing was replaced by laws and judgment, of the need to follow the rules, of reward and punishment and learning how to become outwardly successful, all needed for creating a shell of national success called outer identity. Outer success first came as the creation, stabilization and defense of national borders, but inner conflict within the borders quickly followed. This cycle and pattern was repeated over and over, as endless power struggles and wars for all men of every generation. It had to be that way since life was a matter of life or death struggles within the mind's reality. Then after thousands of years of history there were new stories of transition called healing. New stories of life beyond leaders and followers and winners and losers began.

With the birth of the expanded capacity to love (which is healing), stories began pointing to a dream and destiny beyond the world of power struggles and wars and outer differences that separated and polarized people, to experience **our**story, as a loving, healing and harmonizing story and celebration of life as never before possible. During that phase of the journey many would experience and then forget the power of love, there would be blindness to it, deafness to it, paralysis without it and living dead without it. The stories said there would be many false paths and false truths and false leaders and power struggles between the old reality and the new one, but ultimately only those who understood love and asked specifically for it would find it and break free of the attachment to the old ways and reality and the suffering it created.

But this dream of future personal wholeness through liberated love, was hidden amongst the still emerging capacity to love another and the confusing older messages we were also taught by society as a whole: the mind was good and the body was bad, men were more important and needed to be mental disciplinarians and in charge of life activities and power struggles, and women were less important as the time and need for physical nurturing was over (or so it seemed). Even as a child I intuitively knew and believed differently, yet I became confused by the information held in these stories—unsure what to believe and what to trust. Confused about the reality of the old ways, or the changes and reality of the new? And yet, this was the way it was. The stories, beliefs and the two main recurrent themes of the old way and mental created reality of life at that time: fear and hope (doing it right or wrong, winner or loser, leader or follower, success or failure, past or future, heaven or hell), or the promises of a new, third type of experience. A third way of living would occur the stories said after an apocalyptic crisis of change and the death of the old conditional mental ways of engaging life in a two-dimensional way. A third way that would liberate the heart's full power and its reality for all.

The paradise of mother's love was gone, especially so for boys. It was time to thicken our armor and march and fight for outer success. I learned that in the land of freedoms, dreams and happiness, the secret to outer success was to mentally focus on outer goals and work hard. To push away from feelings, and think superiorly and then any difficulty could be overcome, any desert crossed, any war won. History was my story too, by default. Her-story, less important, or so it was taught. This was what I heard, how I was mentally programmed as a man, and what I would believe was possible. It was the way of the mind, the mental template for outer success that everyone believed in and passed on. It was the way the old world demanded it to be at that time, there was no other way or reality at that time, for men or for women.

And so the day came when my unique dream began as a mental seed opening up, and eventually manifesting as an outer identity and role in a mentally created, controlled and stabilized surface-oriented and limited reality.

I remember feeling something stir inside me when my parents talked of the kindness Dr. Bill had shown them, of the difficult times when he had cared for us without charge.

Perhaps it started with the shine of the faintly green marble steps my feet touched when I first walked up to "Dr. Bill's" office, which had been built inside the town's old post office. The steps, smooth and always polished to a shine, reflected light, and I always walked them slowly and perhaps even reverently.

In the doctor's office, the air was filled with the pungent smell of antiseptics. It all seemed so wonderfully different from the smells of the cows and chickens and the land of the farm where I lived. I was also fascinated by the people in white, who glided back and forth in silence and mystery behind the reception window.

Who are they? What are they doing? I remember wondering as I peered intently into the room, straining to hear something, eager to know what was behind the glass.

When the time came, as I stepped through the door that separated me from the world of cows, chickens, land, farm people and everything I'd previously known, I wasn't sure how to act. It was such a strange place. Then Dr. Bill, a man of medium height with short brownish hair and glasses and a wonderful white coat, smiled at me, and I felt warm inside. Everything would be all right here.

Dr. Bill was always there—to do surgery, to deliver all the babies, to work the emergency room, to take care of the elders, to be there at their deaths. He was always there to help with the difficult times.

Once, I fell while running around a tree near the county fairgrounds, and a piece of glass cut my leg. The gush of blood surprised me. The wound had torn apart my skin, revealing the beautiful glistening of bone, which was something I'd never seen before, something that was inside me, underneath the surface.

It was late on a Saturday afternoon. The stores in town were closed that day, since everyone had gone to the county fair, but my mother took me right to Dr. Bill's office. She knew he would be there to help, and he was.

He pulled the two torn and separated sides of tissue together with black thread, mending it, so that it could heal and be normal again, protecting what was inside. Dr. Bill smiled, and I knew everything would be just fine.

I'm not sure if it was his smile, his touch or his presence, moving like a single, reflected ray of light that so deeply affected and inspired me. But Dr. Bill, was strangely different from other men; he was not a warrior in the usual sense. I wasn't sure what it was, but suddenly he gave me a goal, a vision, a dream that yearned to come true. To be a physician—to be like Dr. Bill—this passion fueled my entire youth. Nothing else mattered. I was sure this would make me happy.

Many years of discipline and constant study followed in order to nourish that vision. Information streamed in to my mind—feeding it and filling it with genetics, cellular biology, embryology, physiology, anatomy, biochemistry, electron microscopy—forming a critical mass of information.

From my mental perspective I strove to understand the structure, function and order of the physical body, as if it was a machine. What was seen and could be verified was real and could be reproduced. I would identify the mental facts in any illness and then battle the symptoms. The temple of the mind, in its high tower, ruled, logic ruled, and all my energy streamed into it to support its growth and reality.

But there was one event that my mind could not understand—it was the way and the workings of the heart. It was the phenomenon of romantic love that marked the glorious beginning of the third stage of human development and third experience of love; when heaven and earth and mind and body that were once split apart in childhood are briefly unified through the heart's presence.

Love once lost earlier in my life, struck me again, when I was a third-year medical student on six south, the medical surgical floor of Milwaukee County Hospital, and brought me another image that changed everything in my life—a vision of beauty and joy that made me forget the trials and tribulations, the successes and failures of the battles I'd been fighting with my mind.

Her name was Janis. She was a surgical nurse with dark skin, a radiant smile and a wondrous body. I didn't know why or how it happened, the gift of this love—I just knew again that it was the greatest thing I'd ever experienced. The very center of my chest ached, and in her presence the whole world looked strangely beautiful. It was the wondrous rebirth of the energetic experience called love.

The old world of the body and mind separated—released.
Heart pressed against heart. Heart to heart.
The unseen center ignited and igniting.
And the garden of life was full and whole again.

My everyday armor had been pierced and for a while my heart was open, and again, life was transformed. I, the warrior and disciplinarian of the mind, and she, the cheerleader and nurturer of the body, came together. Hearts touching without barriers, and everything seemed perfect in the light of the heart's energies that permeated the air. A sense of unity and wholeness pervaded everything. It was so real, so magical, so wonderfully healing. How was it possible? What was this experience that changed everything? Made the world abloom with flowers and poetry and dance and song? That made everything beautiful? And whom was I transformed into that allowed me to sense everything as beautiful, joy-filled and whole? And what was this mystery of discipline and nurturing being united again? Love was healing and healing was love!

The windows to the heart and its reality had been opened briefly, the mysterious energies of unity, deeply and expansively transmitted *and* received between two individuals. It was an energetic experience of unity that was called romantic love.

The warmth in the center of my chest however, would fade with time as the windows closed, and the beauty and the self that experienced it would go to sleep. Hidden inside, that expression of love would have conditions placed on it and over it, as it became a memory, a beautiful memory, but still a memory. A distant sleeping beauty, an experience of the heart to be forgotten, covered with everyday armor as it had to be for reasons yet unknown to me. Hidden until some unknown day in the future when it might open again, just might be revealed again, just might be found again. A past experience and a future hope seen, heard and held in pictures, old love letters, and the many songs and stories of modern society and its confusing fascination with "love" once found and then lost.

Indeed, a past, brief magnificent experience of romantic love, dependent on another, and a future hope and unexplainable yearning for the heart's return and then...

My mind and thinking began to reassert their power and control as my attention, energy and focus returned to my job. Unknowingly the mystery of love and feelings began its disappearance. The power of love faded as the love and need for mental power returned. The force was with the mind and its capacities to stabilize our outer two-dimensional surface oriented reality, as it had to be, to deal with the challenges ahead. The force supported the shift from warriors and cheerleads to Supermen and Superwomen, our Super Surface (outwardly focused and surface armored) Self. The armor supported and safely stored emotional energies underneath and its shiny light reflecting surface precluded any insight into what was happening. The mind split off from the body again: as if love had strangely lost, as if not strong enough to stay, as if needing to be protected by outer armor.

Information began to flow from mind to mind. Scalpels and drugs would battle with the symptoms that showed themselves. We would win; we would conquer. The successful use of antibiotics and vaccines had resulted in the death of deadly illnesses that had plagued humanity for eons. That victory made my colleagues and me believe we could do anything. If the mind could destroy the sources of those illnesses, then surely the potential and power of the mind was limitless. Together, our minds could continue to operate in the same old way. We could battle with and then cure the world of any new diseases and disorders! Indeed the force was with us.

After my residency I became a physician in a small town, where I would become "Dr. Gil" and take care of the families in the community. With a loving partner, a son and a daughter, friends, great colleagues, a home and land by a river filled with wild trout, working long hours, late nights and always being there for my patients, it was the realization of the vision of my youth. There, happiness would come to live. Or so it seemed to me that the story should unfold that way.

And, indeed, it was good.

Yet it was not long thereafter when I became aware that some mysterious crisis and change was beginning. Slowly my dream of happiness, of the way I wanted things to happen, began slipping away. The old kingdom of men, in the role of the thinkers, bonded together with women, the queens, in the role of the feelers, began to change.

Perhaps I keenly sensed it happening the day one of my favorite mothers, Anna, came to the clinic. Five years before, I'd attended the difficult delivery of her baby boy. Seeing her, I was always reminded of a moment, early in her first pregnancy, when we searched for the heartbeat of her child, and the silently shared happiness of the moment when we heard the that first tiny beat of the baby's heart—lub, dub, lub, dub, lub, dub—so faint and so distant. We smiled at each other, in the silence of sharing such a deep connection through that sound and all of the potential it represented. Having listened and waited for so many months, the power and beauty of her role during labor, and later holding her son to her heart—reminding him of its eternal presence, soothing him.

All this flitted through my mind in an instant. Since then she'd had a second child, a daughter who was three. Over the years, her family life had seemed so perfect in its unfolding. Hers seemed like an all-American family—mother and father were always pleasant; the kids were always well dressed and full of smiles, freely giving me hugs. The parents showed every care and desire to be there for their kids. I remembered them embracing each other after the birth of their son, who now looked so much like his father. A father who had a great job and love for his children. A mother with fiery red hair and enthusiasm for life. Anna's eyes always met mine with excitement as she told me what was happening in their home and in their family life.

But this day was different.

Averting her eyes and turning her head away slightly, she sighed and uttered the unthinkable. "We're separating," she said, looking down.

No, that can't be possible, not your family, I thought.

"It just isn't working out," she added.

Why didn't I see it coming? How could I not have known until now? And what about the kids?

As if Anna knew my thoughts, she said, "I'm going to go and live with my mother."

This just isn't right. It just isn't right.

Finally, I managed to mutter, "I'm so sorry. I hope things will work out for you."

But something changed that day—the vision of happiness that had been held for life in our little town and the good life of "Dr. Bill," my childhood hero, began to die...

Months passed, and it seemed every week brought in news that another young couple whose babies I had delivered were divorcing. Even having babies didn't seem to create enough love or reason to stay together.

Soon I grew tired. I was beginning to burn out.

Some kind of crisis was erupting—not of natural illness, of infections, cancer or broken bones. No, this was a crisis that was filled with an intense hunger for more than outer happiness, and it manifested itself as a vast array of new symptoms—symptoms that medical science had never before faced.

However as before, I thought new treatments would always be discovered that would rekindle hope, and I felt renewed by the promises they held. *Yes, we can still win!*

Now I heard myself uttering new diagnoses and treatments, "I'm sorry, but the psychologist said he has 'attention deficit disorder.' But don't worry, a lot of kids have this problem now, and we know how to treat it with medication."

Or I'd say, smiling supportively, "It looks like all of your symptoms are caused by depression. We're not sure why so many people are getting it, but research has shown that it is associated with an imbalance of brain chemicals. We have new medications to treat that imbalance and great counselors, so don't worry."

Or, "So, as I understand it, you can't leave town because every time you get near the city limits, you feel like you might die. It sounds like you're having panic attacks. We're not sure why so many people are suffering from these attacks now, but here's a new medication for that, and we'll get you in for counseling."

Or, "You aren't sleeping well? Well a lot of people seem to be having this problem now, it just so happens we have new medications to help with that..."

And then I saw addictive patterns, which had been ordinarily moderate and well hidden, become more severe and erupt with devastating consequences.

I'd say, "Your body's dying because you aren't eating enough. You need to stop your drug use." And then, ironically, "We have some drugs to help relieve your anxiety and depression..."

Or, "It looks like your daughter will recover from the overdose. Thank God she didn't hit a tree when she fell asleep behind the wheel. We'll get her in to counseling..."

Or, "Your addiction to alcohol is ruining your life. We can give you medicine that makes you violently sick with intense vomiting when you drink. That might help. Better yet, let's get you into Alcoholics Anonymous. They have one of the best programs for this..."

Suddenly, a way of life and the traditional roles of men and women in the family that had been changing slowly over thousands of years were now being stressed and changing rapidly. It was no longer enough for men to be just warriors and disciplinarians and women just cheerleaders and nurturers. What confusion, anger and power struggles these changes created!

Our friends began to get divorced, depressed or change jobs—all searching for something else. Things weren't supposed to be this way. Everyone seemed hungry in a way I couldn't understand, yearning for *more*—but more of what? Something had to be done.

I saw physical obesity as it was just starting to become a widespread issue of concern. Though initially rare, of all the new addictions, the addiction to food was most easy to see and treat—or so I thought. So I focused on treating that issue first. Yet despite great effort, employing the tactics of fear and hope, I saw only minimal success. Ultimately, very few with this condition sought me out.

Then Bob, the local Alcoholics Anonymous counselor came to my office. In his 50s, with a large round belly and partly bald, he always wore a white shirt with the collar open and a gray-checkered sports jacket. Generally, he seemed the epitome of good cheer and optimism, but this day was different. This day he was spitting a fire mixed with anger and frustration. He was on a rampage to get people off alcohol.

"Gil," he spat, "I need you to scare the living daylights out of these drinkers. If we can scare them enough, they'll stop. I want you to tell them what alcohol can do to their bodies."

My mind energized immediately with tactics I was sure would bring victory over this addiction. Bob's call had given me a new sense of purpose and meaning. We would beat alcoholism. Once again I would use the only tools we had, the powerful tools of fear of what would happen physically and hope of what we mentally could do to fight the enemy. Mental willpower would win.

I was invigorated with the excitement of fighting and winning this war!

Shortly after his call, I stepped into the AA meeting hall prepared to create sheer dread of alcohol. This was the demon to get rid of, and once I'd scared those present sufficiently with fear, I'd give them hope and the promise of a better life, a *normal* life without alcohol. Yes, we—they—would win!

More than 20 people, all looking like tired warriors, sat around the periphery of the room on the few cloth lounge chairs and the many metal chairs mixed in between.

I saw one man I knew in the far left corner. He was in his mid-50s and in the last stages of cirrhosis of the liver. He reclined in a chair, his abdomen swollen from accumulated water because his liver was blocking the flow of blood and water from below. The skin and the whites of his eyes were yellow due to a buildup of bilirubin, which is a natural substance created from the breakdown of old blood cells that is ordinarily released by the liver. In this case, however, his diseased liver couldn't release the bilirubin, and its levels in him were growing toxic. He'd be dead within a few months. I knew these meetings were precious to him. He wanted to be with others as he prepared for death, and yet a part of him, he'd told me in private, still hoped he might get better.

A patient of mine sat to the right. Now bankrupt, unemployed and estranged from his wife, there was no work for him, no home to go to at the end of the day and no wife to nurture or hold him. He had a newborn daughter, but she was now fatherless and would be waiting forever for her father. He wouldn't be there to embrace her—ever; he couldn't break the restraining order his wife had taken out against him.

"I know they'll be better off without me," he had said many times in my office, where he released some of his pain. Over and over, he tried to gain freedom from his dependence on alcohol. One day not long after this, filled with guilt and pain, he left town altogether, lost in the ocean of human tragedies.

And there were many others, emaciated and "dry," socializing, their battle with alcoholic spirits seemingly complete. They all had "war stories" to share, even laughs, and they had each other. They were comrades and veterans in the greatest-unrecognized war that was affecting all of us in so many ways.

My mind honed in on what their personal demon was doing to them. I would point the finger at the enemy, and by eliminating the enemy we would win the greatest of wars. So I began forcefully:

"Even a small amount of alcohol on a regular basis can kill those who are susceptible. It's always killing brain cells and liver cells." I continued, stressing how the alcohol did its damage and how cells actually died, carefully avoiding mention of those in the group who were already dying from it.

The program that followed included discussion and a time for questions and answers. Some spoke of friends and relatives whose problems were much worse than theirs. Some told of their past struggles with alcohol. They were now free, but guarded about the future, never knowing when temptation would strike again—when or where the enemy would show up—in a bottle, on a billboard, in a TV ad with laughing happy people surrounding bottles of liquor. I thought, *How confusing this war is.*

As my monthly meetings with the AA group continued, old warriors who thought they were cured left, to be replaced by new veterans. The crisis continued, and the war continued. Increasingly, people revealed that they were fighting multi-drug addictions along with alcohol, which by itself was no longer addiction enough to fill their needs.

Soon, I was seeing their sons and daughters—children who had the same addictions as their parents, plus new ones. New wars were being declared regularly. Following a war on alcohol was a war on smoking, then a war on drugs, a war on obesity, a war on gambling and a war on pornography.

At the same time, the medical community began its own wars, which were often related to their unsuccessful wars on the addictions. There was a war on high blood pressure, a war on diabetes, a war on cancer, a war on cholesterol, a war on heart disease, and on and on. Everyone had a cause and a war to be involved in, or so it seemed.

Most of our efforts in the wars seemed to contain the enemy somewhat, but in reality, in whatever war, the enemy simply disguised itself and returned as a different addiction.

However, there seemed to be one amazing success story—the war against touch! Whether applied to teachers, clergy, counselors or medical personnel, the rule was confusing. In order to avoid any touch that might be sexual, or any touch that might be construed as condescending or authoritarian, touch became a legal issue. As physicians, we were taught and advised that only analytical, clinical touch was acceptable—that's how it needed to be.

Nurturing through touch, which had been integral to human life for centuries was also being lost. Clinical touch only? Cold, hard, objective touch only—like touching a car to evaluate it? Only this available? Where was this all going?

This loss of touch was, I noticed, unconsciously spilling over to parents and the way they confusingly interacted with their children. Touch that nurtured or disciplined was being lost. Men especially were becoming more and more isolated from their capacity to receive touch, even feeling awkward. How were they supposed to touch now? Confusion about touch was accelerating. Feelings coming from the body were also increasingly guarded against as being "unmanly."

Women, too, began to question the value of touch, feelings and nurturing, as the world of the mind called and seemed more important. The world of the mind, thinking and outer power and values became more important than the body and its deeper feelings. The mind was trying to take full control of the body and life. A strange emptiness on the inside and a separation from feelings was beginning and simultaneously an explosion of new addictions and illicit drug use began.

An explosion of new prescription drugs, diets, supplements, therapies and ways to cope and win was also occurring. The number of books with laws, secrets, keys, doorways and pathways that promised mental success, to mentally focus and win, to vanquish whatever the enemy, seemed endless. The hunger for them seemed limitless.

"Our fears can be put behind us and our hopes of winning and living the good life can become reality," they all said. It was a simple matter of mind over body, of mind over addiction. It all sounded good, yet an endless war had begun. We argued in the medical profession that we were winning, but in reality we were losing. We remained blind and deaf to the fact that everyone was simply switching from one form of addiction to another. Some were even addicted to avoiding old addictions, directing all their life force and energy to avoiding the addiction and the people, circumstances and places associated with their former addiction.

We had no new understanding of what was happening. Just old tools (drugs, goal setting and talk therapies etc.) in different forms, but with the same old belief that we were in a war with symptoms and that as supermen and superwomen we could mentally win.

I too was still trying to hold on to the dream of happiness and the ability to control and fix things. The dream that had been instilled in me many years ago in a time of youthful innocence and idealism—a time when I still thought my mind could solve all of the world's problems. I held on to being Dr. Gil for as long as I could, until a nagging sense of something missing crept into me—an uninvited and unexplainable yearning for something more.

Amid so much to be thankful for, I began to struggle with my job. What had once been my dream and my life's purpose became something I struggled with and battled against daily. I was deeply and privately confused. I did not share the existence of this struggle—hoping it would resolve itself, but something was wrong, something profound was missing. Sometimes the struggle came as an intense hunger for more, as if a part of me knew there was something profoundly beautiful waiting for me, and sometimes as an intense yearning to break free, as if I were somehow imprisoned. But what was imprisoned and how?

Then an unexpected crisis arrived. What had nourished me and what I'd pursued and achieved during the first half of my life, what my mind had striven so hard to create, what had seemed to be the crowning achievement of my life—wasn't enough. That day, the young boy's dream of the happiness brought by the white coat came to an abrupt end. Happiness (things happening to go my way) wasn't enough. The white coat wasn't enough.

It was my 40th birthday, and something had to change. That day I said, "I have to leave my work. I'm not sure why. All I know is, I must leave."

My life as "Dr. Bill," the small town family physician, had come to an end.

The clinic was empty on my last night as I cleaned out my desk. In it were 11 years' worth of cards and pictures. One, from Julie, a single mother whose delivery I'd attended, made me pause. The card pictured her three-year-old daughter with a blue ribbon in her blonde hair. Julie's hope and love were held in that child. Her note said, "Thank you so much. I'll never forget that day." I remembered the birth and Julie's fierce determination to raise the child on her own—to make a better life for her daughter, and I hoped it could be so.

The door leading out of the clinic opened. I stepped through and tried to remain tough, but regret swept over me—regret that I would feel for many years—regret that I hadn't filled the birth room of every newborn child with flowers and music, so that, at the moment of emergence, flowers would greet the child— flowers of many different colors and sweet fragrances—and music, Handel's *Messiah:* "Alleluia, Alleluia, A...lle...lu...ia," and Beethoven's *Ode to Joy.* It just seemed to me that it should be that way.

Maybe someday it will be that way for every birth, I thought, as the automatic door to the clinic clicked and locked behind me.

That missing something I couldn't find through work had suddenly become extremely important, more important than anything else in life.

Leaving the life I'd lived, the families I'd been with through so much, my dedicated colleagues and my social life, was hard. But the yearning to understand what "ails us all" was now more important to me. Something profound was missing in our lives and its absence was making us sick. Something so profound and so deep and so expansive, that my mind could not yet grasp it, but it would try. I didn't have any other way to approach it.

I shifted my life, becoming an ER physician, which freed up time to read about alternative aspects of medicine, psychology and energy dynamics (a vision of the body as a complex of energy and energy fields that interact with each other). Gradually I came to understand the fundamental differences between *curing* (mentally controlling, cutting out or fixing symptoms we could see and identify), which was the medical model I had been taught, and *healing* (restoring and bringing inner balance to life), an energetic reality difficult for my mind to comprehend, much less create.

I felt like an immigrant learning a new language—a language of energy, energy dynamics and healing, which included words and ideas that were new to me—chakras, meridians, currents, energy centers, energy fields, matrix, fusion, in the flow, synergy, burned out, wired, feeling high and feeling low (on energy), zoned out (blocked energy), turned on, turned off, transformers (changing energy from one form to another), transmission and reception of energy.

At that time I was especially grateful for a new friend I had met—Dave, a heart surgeon, who for years had been on the same journey I was now taking. We'd both regularly attended conferences by fellow physician Brugh Joy, on the heart center as an energetic source of healing, a process engaged in part by Eastern Medicine. Dave and I were moved by these conferences and the concepts of a new model of healing for our patients and us. We were exploring the frontiers of medicine and the shift from curing alone to curing integrated with healing potentials.

The concepts introduced deepened my understanding of the body as not only a mass of cells, but as being a mass of organized energy, with specific energy centers called *chakras*. Each of these seven energy centers expresses itself according to the amount of energy flowing through it. With time, however, I began to see the seven more simply as three major energy centers, called the mind center for thinking, the body center for feeling and the heart center for loving/unity. Health was a matter of internally connecting to and balancing mind and body with the full presence of the heart.

Unlike at other conferences, at these we were taught to shift and expand our awareness so we could "feel and sense" the energy coming from within our bodies. In time, it was simple to sense, and even on occasion, to see these fields coming from everyone. What was once a weak belief, concept and information, I now felt and experienced inside myself as real and increasingly integrated.

With turning on my heart, my body became alive and my hands began to feel different. Sometimes they became very warm just after my chest began to feel warm. With my hands, I could feel the energy of the heart center and the other energy centers that extended out about a foot or two from my body and that of others. Just as energy transformed to heat is invisible, yet can be felt, so, too, can these fields be sensed and felt. With time it was easy for me to feel and simultaneously see the energy coming off the tips of my fingers, like small lights.

I had now more fully entered the second half of my life and the energy world of Einstein. I began to realize that the simple act of focusing on my heart not only rejuvenated me but also resulted in the capacities to explore life, in a way that was never possible before. I was now really getting outside the box or matrix of my black and white mental world.

Through group processes during which everyone focused their awareness on the center in the middle of the chest (the "Heart Chakra"), a field of unifying energy was created for all. This "turning on/being aware" increasingly gave us the wisdom, love and courage to explore our "inside stuff" and move through years and years of personal issues.

Unlike the profoundly beautiful, but unconsciously experienced, brief reality of romantic love with one other, I was now waking up to consciously see life as a different self, through different eyes and experiencing a completely different reality (an emerging experience of love of self and all of life).

Filled with heart's energies to overflowing, I fell into unexpected moments of awe at the beauty of the life surrounding me.

It began by looking at a cluster of small pink flowers on a desert bush. Suddenly I wept over the intense beauty, and found myself asking "How is it possible I didn't see or know about this before."

Tears of joy came over and over again during the first day of my awakening, as the beauty now seen and heard and touched was so gracious and so radiant. During the following days my experience of radiance, mellowed into a state of quiet gratitude to life.

This way of being with life was truly beyond the ordinary understanding of my energy naïve old self.

A transformed state of unconditional love, a healing presence, innate harmony and compassion was no longer a future possibility, but becoming an embodied experience in the here and now.

I began to see our lives as epic journeys, as reflected in all the ancient and modern stories of the four stages of life and human development.

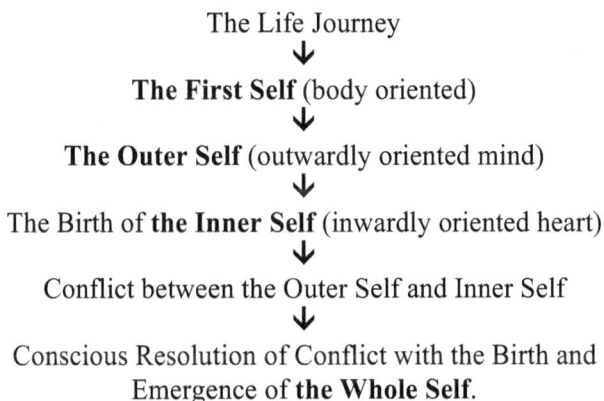

The Life Journey
↓
The First Self (body oriented)
↓
The Outer Self (outwardly oriented mind)
↓
The Birth of **the Inner Self** (inwardly oriented heart)
↓
Conflict between the Outer Self and Inner Self
↓
Conscious Resolution of Conflict with the Birth and
Emergence of **the Whole Self**.

First Half of Life-Outwardly Referenced
Stage One: The body, feelings and nurturing.
Stage Two: The mind, thinking and discipline.
Second Half of Life-Inwardly Referenced
Stage Three: The heart, loving and healing.
Stage Four: The soul, joy and wholeness.

I realized that when I was involved in stage two and its reality, I was outwardly focused and had little awareness of stage three and its reality, beyond the experience of romantic love. I also realized that the inner journey through stage three was not easy until the unifying energy would be more fully liberated and stage four and its reality could be experienced more and more (outer and inner integrated as wholeness).

It was natural to suffer because of holding on to old ways, while simultaneously yearning for the new ways. It would continue until we could understand life energetically and open the door and fully liberate love (the experience of unity and wholeness). We were called to walk with others on this inner yellow brick road, to go from confusion to wisdom, from emptiness to heartfulness and from fear to the courage to change.

Called to come home, to rejuvenate our lives with a life transforming energy and the inherent joy of its liberation!

During these conferences, I felt excited and changed as the experience of centering was embodied more and more fully on the inside and also revealed more completely outside of me. My intellectual understanding was giving way to intermittent experiences of "wholeness." As the "transformed self," I felt immense gratitude for the gift of my life over and over again.

However, within weeks of returning home, old patterns of living returned. This was especially true at work. The mental reality and intensities of life returned, the "same old, same old" patterned behavior began, and I was again a medical warrior in white armor, battling symptoms and working strictly out of my mind (and split off from my body and feelings), alongside other medical warriors doing the same. Warriors all unknowingly experiencing a thickening of their armor and increasing disconnection from their hearts.

The warmth in my chest that had been felt so much during the conference began to slowly fade, and with time, it would disappear. My contact with Dave became an important reminder of the heart's energies and I was delighted to have a fellow physician and traveler with me as we explored the inspiring journey ahead, to even deeper and more expansive experiences of centering and the unifying experience also known as liberated unconditional love. Unknowingly it would begin with tragedy.

4

Emptiness

*With outer successfulness comes the realization
of our inner emptiness.*

April 3, 1993:

"It was a horrible crash," Bob, a fellow emergency room physician working in a nearby ER, said over the phone. "Gil, I thought of you right away. I knew Dave was a friend of yours, thought you ought to know. Dave just died. We tried to bring him back, but the injuries were too much."

Bob went on to describe the events that had taken place in those dark, early morning hours. Then he added something strange, "Gil, someone said he was waving his left hand outside of his car window some time before the crash."

Perhaps he was trying to wake himself up, I thought.

I could see Dave in my mind's eye—his striking presence, tall, piercing eyes and long black hair held back in a ponytail. I could see him behind the wheel of the green Volvo station wagon, moving through the darkness and silence of the morning, trying to stay awake, to go on, but his mind and body were so tired they yearned for sweet sleep. I could see his eyelids so heavy they had to close, and his head nodding off, punctuated by a few last jerks as he tried to stay awake. I could see his car suddenly cross the centerline of the road. Then, the oncoming headlights, the screeching wheels of the semi, then steel exploding against steel, metal rushing inward, crashing against Dave's body, his chest and his heart.

Bob said, "There were no last words. We struggled with a crushed chest, worked on him for an hour."

But Dave didn't want to stay. He couldn't stay, I thought to myself. *What irony—a heart surgeon dying of heart wounds.*

I felt Dave's huge presence again: outgoing, handsome, charming and engaging. He was always adventurous, encouraging and daring. Arriving at work on his black Harley Davidson motorcycle, wearing a black leather cap, yet able to

50

transform into his patients' endearing physician. He'd been at the epitome of success in his outer life, and at times I even envied him.

He'd kept a secret, however, that not even his very best friends were aware of, that I only learned of later. Behind his everyday persona of confidence and complete success, Dave was undergoing a deep private struggle with the darkness of depression. Like so many, he, too, was searching for something else, something elusive, just out of his reach.

I remembered once, while we were talking over lunch, he paused, his eyes shifting momentarily to the right as if seeing some distant image. Then he smiled and began talking about a retreat center he would help build in northern California for teaching the new and unfolding models for healing. But, shortly after our meeting, his dream of building that healing center, that Shangri La, collapsed, and a part of Dave died with the dream.

He continued serving—cutting open chests, touching and repairing physical hearts. But his yearning continued for that something else, as did his very secret and difficult struggle with depression…

My awareness returned to the phone conversation I was presently having with Bob. I realized that I was reacting no differently than I would to a report of any other death in the Emergency Room. It was just another fact, another clinical event. I had no feelings, no emotions about it.

Bob said, "It was hard, Gil. So much damage—chest injuries, abdominal injuries. He never regained consciousness." Bob and I talked for a while about Dave's family, who had already left ahead of him for a vacation in Mexico and were not yet aware of his death.

Our conversation then switched to the "politics" at his hospital and mine. "No," I said, "things are never going to be the same."

We agreed, as we had in many such conversations in the past, that the politics of medicine were on the wrong track, that medicine was becoming too mechanical, that something was missing, and that it was out of our control to fix it.

"Thanks for calling me," I said. I hung up, and I returned to the quiet of our kitchen.

I stood alone, staring at the brown quarry tile, emotionless and empty. Death was touching me now, making life empty and meaningless, sucking me dry; there wasn't a single tear, no sense of loss. Within the outer shell of who and what I believed myself to be, I found complete emptiness—a dark abyss.

How could this be? Had I no feelings for this person I'd grown so very fond of? Dave had been a good friend, a confidant, and someone who also intensely yearned for change. How could this be?

Death was insisting I look at it. Only emptiness looked back.

I thought, *Have I reached the point in my life where I have no feelings?*

Janis appeared and asked, "What's happened, Gil?"

I told her about Bob's call in exacting detail—the timing and the clinical events surrounding the injuries; the crushed chest and fractured ribs; and the final cause of death, direct trauma to the heart, causing it to fail.

Compassion overcame Janis, and she wept deeply—not only for Dave, but also for Dave's family, who were still unaware of what had happened. I stood by, as if in the emergency room, outwardly understanding and supportive, but inside myself stoic, with no emotion, none, nothing.

Minutes passed. Janis paused and then looked at me in confusion and frustration. "Is there something wrong with you?" she said sharply. Then she turned and left the room.

She was right. Something was wrong. It was as if I didn't care that Dave had died. It was as if I didn't care at all. Had all my capacities to feel and to love been lost? Had medicine and my mental preoccupation with the search for the something missing led only to this?

I was a successful dead man walking, trapped in the white metal armor of success. I was the authority of my outer world, but without feeling, empty and dark, without a heart. Suddenly, I was lost—blind to any path ahead. There was nothing to focus on.

Dave had searched and searched, too, and yet it seemed he had not found the answer. Would my search also come without an answer, only to end with physical death?

Indeed, the cost of finding the answer would be more deaths—more strange deaths.

5

Shauna Lee

Our dying bodies and confused minds
are waiting for our hearts to awaken us.

Death was hiding in a beautiful day.

The sun's early morning rays cut through the canopy of evergreen branches, creating patterns of light and dark on the ground just outside my hospital call room window.

I'd mostly forgotten yesterday—the day of Dave's death. I had stored it away like a bad dream, deep into my unconscious, behind the white coat. I was back at work; doing what needed to be done, mind fully in control again.

It was a slow Sunday morning in the ER, and I was preparing to return to my call room and enjoy the soft breeze that I knew was moving through its open window. There I could return once again to my fervent love of reading anything and everything that pertained to healing. My mind, having recovered, was back on track, and I resumed the mental quest for the answer to the missing something that would restore purpose to life and push the emptiness away.

It was Palm Sunday, just one week before Easter, and the churches in town were filled; I expected things would be quiet until they let out.

I was walking through the ER when a message crackled over the old intercom: "Small girl fell out of a hayloft and landed on her head on the concrete below." She was unconscious and not breathing; her father had begun mouth-to-mouth resuscitation. The nursing staff began preparing for a serious head injury. The paramedics had already called the helicopter from the regional trauma center in to flight. Serious trauma demanded quick action, and the flight crew would arrive in thirty minutes or so.

I tried to feel my way into the scenario that might unfold. If she regained consciousness here, it was possible she could stay in this facility under observation, but if she was more seriously injured or death seemed likely, the helicopter crew would be ready to transfer her.

While waiting for the arrival of the ambulance, I settled in for a few more pages of reading and searching in the quiet. The sirens came quickly. As they got louder and louder, I closed my book and hurried back to the ER.

The paramedics and EMTs came bursting through the ambulance garage door and rushed down the corridor to the ER. On the stretcher was four-year-old Shauna Lee, blonde, pageboy haircut, eyes closed, still unconscious.

As they wheeled her in to the trauma room, next to the nurse's station, I stepped in behind them. Nurses rushed in, making assessments, taking vitals: blood pressure, pulse rates, respiratory rates and mental status. They started IVs, hooked up monitors, put in a urinary catheter, drew blood and did whatever else needed to be done immediately.

I began my clinical examination of her body. She lay still, her knees together and drawn up halfway and with her hips twisted to the right. Her upper torso was twisted toward the left, her arms lay slightly away from the sides of her body, her eyes were closed and her head was slightly tilted to the left. She seemed so vulnerable, so innocent and death-like, except for occasional, slight muscular twitches in her arms. I could see no other visible or palpable trauma other than to her head.

Yet her body spoke deeply to me—it was as if she was more than just another body. Suddenly it was as if she was divine. It was as if the fate of the world itself rested within her.

Then the nurse gently laid a small, white, blue-speckled gown over her body, covering the mystery of what was sensed in the moment.

Just then her body shuddered, and my body started shuddering—touching all of me, changing something, beginning to tear me apart.

But I shook off the vision and feeling. The ER needed a physician with outer, not inner, vision. I needed to attend to the outer duty—be in control, hold it together, do what needed to be done, and swiftly.

Shauna Lee would have to be intubated. Clearly she'd suffered significant brain injury—she'd been unconscious for too long. We needed to paralyze her and then breathe for her, so she'd make no more movements. Any movement might increase bleeding or increase swelling in the brain, and this would worsen the outcome, and even possibly result in death. The tube would also protect her from aspiration, since vomiting is common in head injuries; the stomach's contents can easily go into the lungs, which crucially needed protection.

Anxiety crept into me.

Shauna Lee groaned softly, almost silently, a few times.

Suddenly, her left arm straightened and moved spontaneously behind her left side.

No, not this! Not this!

Her left hand twisted inward and up, repeatedly, her head arched backwards, her neck contracted, over and over...

"Posturing!" I snapped. This was a disastrous sign that Shauna Lee's brain injury was more severe than I'd originally suspected, the damage to the brain so intense any meaningful recovery would be nearly impossible. Images streamed into my mind: paralysis, bedsores, bedridden 24/7, her small body being turned every hour, slurred speech, unable to hold her head up, a wheelchair...

And now I would be a part of creating this tragedy, by trying to keep her alive!

Her eyes remained closed. Her little body was dwarfed by the big ER trauma cart. One of the paramedics tested her eyes for any sign of reaction to light to see if her brain was functioning properly. Her pupils were large and sluggish, her eyes drifted to the side. *Not good, not good at all...*

But that didn't matter.

They were blue eyes, and at that moment that mattered, more than anything. *Oh, God,* that mattered!

And her hair: straight, blonde, pageboy-cut—that mattered. *Oh, God,* that mattered!

The promises held in that body, the joy that child knew of, the hope that child held—those promises and hopes were mine, too! And they were lying there, dying.

Nothing else mattered now, absolutely nothing.

Precious breath, precious life.

My body reacted—some explosion ready to happen inside me.

Stirring inside from my inner abyss, a question emerged: *Will you allow yourself to feel? Will you allow yourself to open up?*

And the answer came: *Yes, this time I will feel.* The yearning and ache pressing so urgently from within me gave me no other choice.

Little did I understand the implications of that decision—to move directly from the familiar outer world of intellect and logic into the world of feelings and emotions, to step through the barrier between ER physician to human being with feelings. Though the white coat still covered me, the role it carried and the protection it gave began to disappear. Uncertainty rushed in, washing down, over and through my body, weakening my muscles, tightening my gut, making my chest ache, my throat constrict...

One of the nurses looked directly at me, and her voice pierced through the fog of uncertainty she must have perceived in me. She brought the message that we would, without failure, proceed.

"Doctor, it's time," she said, and she opened the intubation kit and its medications that would paralyze our little girl. During that brief following moment, when she would become totally limp and her breath would stop, I'd be expected to place a small tube through her mouth and into her trachea so "we" could begin breathing for her.

But my hesitation intensified, and the crowd of medical personnel in the room amplified it with frozen stares of anticipation.

All eyes fixed on Shauna Lee—every breath stopped, every heart pounded as we hovered over Shauna Lee. Everyone else in the room wanted to help, and yet no one was able to hold and guide my hand...

Suddenly the circle of people grew; more poured through the ER door. They, too, needed to be there, as if called, as if their own fate rested on the outcome of this sudden, unexpected emergency.

Now the circle was three-deep; a little girl lay alone in its center, a few last twitches away from being lifeless, awaiting fate. The burden of the outcome settled inside me now. I knew the signs, and I knew the prognosis.

"Doctor, it's time," the nurse repeated insistently as the paralyzing agent coursed through Shauna Lee's veins, rushing to every muscle.

"Doctor, it's time!" she exclaimed sharply, and this time her words broke through my own paralysis.

I awoke, stepped to the head of the bed and crouched down closer to the child.

Her breath turned shallow, as if her last were near. Her chest rose and fell less and less, and then it barely moved.

Looking down on her, I became aware of my own breath softly falling over her face, of her closed eyes, her short blonde hair, her innocence, dying.

Beyond human now, she was divinity in flesh.

Gratitude for the gift of the body and life swept over me. Her body was no longer an object—how could a miracle, a life, be an object?

How to be with this body now?

My mind spun, confused. Conflicted, all that had been learned and done by my mind in the past was unable to comprehend the present yearning to grasp a different reality and understanding of the presence of this divine, human body. My hand hesitated in its movement. How to be with her body now? How to touch with compassion? To touch a world beyond the ordinary outer reality and surface armor I was accustomed to? Beyond the clinical touch I'd known?

But then *grace* descended.

Emerging through my confusion and fear, guiding my right hand toward Shauna Lee's right cheek. My mind, demanding to stay in charge, told me, *You're only stabilizing her face for the intubation.*

But my heart and hand had become one. My soul knew more of this offering, and my hand touched her right cheek.

Flesh—igniting divinity.
Divinity—igniting flesh.

Like the first rays of morning, light burst forth, piercing through my white coat, cracking my armor of resistance, sending shock waves through my body.

And then...

Her chest stopped moving, and her body went limp.

Beep, beep, beep... the heart monitor's rhythm broke the silence. *Beep, beep, beep...* the only sound of life. *Beep, beep, beep...* blood flowed, unseen, supporting Shauna Lee's life silently as she descended into another world.

My right hand now firmly rested against her cheek; a nurse placed the laryngoscope in my left hand. It's cold, silvery metal handle held batteries for a tiny light near the end of a curved metal blade. The blade would go into the child's mouth, under the tongue, to pull up her chin so I could insert the plastic tube I would then hold in my right hand. This was an easy procedure under ordinary circumstances, something I'd done many times before, but on this day, I felt drained and uncertain...

A totally irrational guilt then swept over me: *I'm responsible for this little girl's injury and fate.* I was responsible for the outcome because I hadn't been able to feel, responsible for this tragedy because I was on duty. I had failed; I hadn't done something right. Maybe life or something else was punishing me for not feeling, and now an innocent child would suffer...

What if she survives? Can I live with myself, knowing what that survival would look like, knowing I'd been part of creating such a compromised life?

I had no choice. The paralyzing agent had passed through her body, and her breath was gone. Only one task remained: put the tube in.

I'd seen legs torn off by trains, smashed heads with brains oozing out from motorcycle accidents, bodies burned to a crisp—I'd been there and done what I had to do, but I'd faced nothing so difficult as this moment of feeling such a strange guilt and responsibility for the event.

I felt drained, unable to move. And then another part of me took over and slipped the blade into the now lax mouth, behind the tongue and lifted the jaw up, revealing the moist, pink, delicate inner passages. The plastic tube followed the blade's light, the tube's tip moving slowly toward the tiny pink ring that marked the opening of the dark passage into Shauna Lee's lungs. The tube slipped in easily and down toward the center of the chest to just above where the one main passage split into two. Then the metal blade came out, her jaw relaxed, the paralyzed mouth and lips closing around the tube.

A nurse secured the tube with tape that was then placed over Shauna Lee's cheeks. Air coursed into the tube, into both the right and left lungs, which rose simultaneously with the paramedic's first squeeze of the resuscitation bag. The breath sounds were checked; yes, both sides sounded fine. The cyclic hiss of the squeezed resuscitation bag continued: *breath in, breath out, hiss, pause, hiss, pause, hiss, pause…*

Medication was ordered to help reduce the swelling of the brain. *It might help a little; it might also be just enough to keep her tragically alive.*

The helicopter crew from the nearby trauma center was now in the room and took over.

Shauna Lee laid quietly, no longer twitching and giving false hope. The medical personnel closed in around her, and she disappeared in the circle of bodies. I pulled away, retracting farther and farther in to the distant corner of the trauma room, away from the powerful ER light that beamed down on Shauna Lee from above. Pressing the back of my body against the wall's cool green tiles for support, I felt alone again, fearful and weak, as if in death's presence.

Her family was waiting for me in the hallway outside the room; I had one more task. *What to do? What can I possibly say to the parents of this beautiful little girl? Can I tell them of her true fate?*

There were many family members. Shauna Lee's mother and six-year-old sister had blonde hair, like hers. *What will it be like for her sister to be alone without Shauna Lee? And the father: will he feel responsible for the fall his daughter took? How their lives will change!*

Shauna Lee, this little girl, had broken through my armor and into my emptiness, touching something deep and precious and painful. Now hopelessness invaded me, and for the first time in my professional life, I didn't know what to do next. I only knew one thing: the center of my chest ached so much.

Breathe, Gil. Concentrate on your breath. Regain your composure.

I swallowed slowly several times, releasing the ache and tightness in my throat, getting it back down to where it had come from. I looked at the family and heard myself say, "Come, and let's make a circle."

In the hallway in front of the Emergency Room Nursing Station, outside the trauma room, we stood, hand reaching for hand creating a healing circle: grandma, grandpa, mother, father, sister and friends.

I said, "Shauna Lee has had a brain injury. Let's ask that she be... supported in her journey."

I couldn't use the word *saved,* because I knew it wouldn't happen. I couldn't give false hope; I was aware of no force that could save her. Her fate was sealed—I knew it.

We stood silently, hand in hand. My private thoughts I kept to myself, like the private battles inside me. My mind and the forces of rationality trying to control, to fix, to hold things together, pushing against the sensations and aching and heat in my chest and the weakness of my body.

Feelings were becoming unfrozen, the waters starting to flow. The straining dam inside me was beginning to leak. I was sure it would burst if I gave voice to the truth of Shauna Lee's fate. Inside me, the fight continued, forces demanding attention, battling against forces demanding silence and a return to a "good" day—a rational, mentally controlled, normal day.

Farther down the hall and behind us, the ER trauma doors swung open. The cart emerged, and we all turned. The helicopter crew and ambulance attendants surrounding the cart stopped, and we, on our side of the cart, parted.

And there... hope lay lifeless, alone in the center of the white cloth.

Shauna Lee's mother left the circle, walked slowly toward her child and stopped at the left side of the cart. There lay her child, whom she'd nourished inside, carried inside, loved inside of her. Her child, who had known the rhythm of her mother's heartbeat and breath deep inside every cell. Her child, who had held the hope and the promise of so much love.

Her mother's left hand moved toward her child, gently touching Shauna Lee's right temple, then resting there, her fingers slowly stroking the golden hair one last time.

Her mother's eyes closed as she bent down and kissed Shauna Lee's forehead, mother's kiss descending like a faint strand of light through darkness, through the depths and into the realm of the impossible... to touch...

My heart ached; my armor against feeling was being torn at again and again. Something wanted to be birthed. *But not in the ER, Gil. Suck it up! Suck it back inside. Be tough. You're in charge of the ER. Chin up!*

My veneer of success returned again, and I took firm hold of an air of confidence. We followed Shauna Lee out of the hospital ER, and the ache within me subsided as we stepped into the warm sunlight.

The helicopter service was new to our town, and a crowd of over 100 people of all ages had gathered around the periphery of the cleared parking lot. Children waited on their bikes, and a few dogs panted, all were watching the helicopter in the center of the lot open its doors.

On a stretcher, the little body of Shauna Lee broke through the outer circle of onlookers, family, medical personnel and strangers surrounding her, leaving everything behind as she crossed the parking lot. The cold, green womb of the helicopter received her; then its metal doors closed tightly, denying our eyes their last connection with hope.

Now the helicopter's blades cut through the air, faster and faster. Dust, leaves and debris left from last fall and winter stirred up again, flying into the crowd.

Protecting my eyes with my left hand and turning away, I looked straight in to the waiting eyes of Shauna Lee's mother, and into her well of grief. Seeing her tears, my tears came, too. No force could hold these back, my first tears as a physician.

I said, "I'm sorry. I'm so sorry... I couldn't do anything else." We embraced, tears flowing. Then we turned and stood arm in arm, looking upward through our tears into the bright sun at the rising helicopter. Shauna Lee was disappearing, disappearing, disappearing, and then was lost in the bright heavens above.

She's gone.

Another wave of energy welled up inside me. I had to regain my composure. *Gil, it's only a few steps into the ambulance garage and back up the ramp, back "home" to the safety and familiarity of the ER.*

Inside, Fran, my friend, fellow volleyball player and emergency room nurse, stood in the hallway. "Are you okay?" he said.

I smiled, "Sure, I'm fine. No problem here. Who's next?" I'd wiped away the tears only Shauna's mother had seen, leaving nothing on my face to shame me in the eyes of others. I still held onto toughness.

A long day and night remained to my shift. As I moved past the ER, my legs felt weak again. I was suddenly so tired, as if I'd walked a lifetime on a long dry path. I knew I was tired of the armor, tired of being a good warrior, tired of the heavy burdens I really hadn't felt fully until then.

Feeling light-headed, I leaned my back against the cold, green-tiled wall and slid down, and tears flowed once more. I tried to breathe through them, tried to get enough air in to my chest to stop them, but lost the battle. Fran waited and watched as I struggled to keep it together, then pulled me up and held me up as we walked toward the call room just down the hall.

When we reached the room, I wept fully. Guilt flooded in again for all the events of the morning, irrational guilt that Shauna Lee had injured herself; guilt over my inability to change the course of events, to control what was happening and save her...

Fran watched calmly and silently from a chair. Only much later did he reveal his concern that I was emotionally "going off the deep end."

I pulled out and read aloud to Fran something I'd written earlier that morning and had stuffed in a pocket of my coat: "The hourglass of life—so much life moves through that narrow piece. How rarely we spend time seeing it because it moves through so quickly. So many precious, beautiful jewels move through that narrow space untouched."

My hands became fists that I now shook in front of my chest. "Why don't we grab life more deeply—grab those precious moments? Why can't we see it? How can we simply let life go through our hands like sand, so quickly?"

Someone had called Janis, my most trusted counselor and confidant, and now, through the darkness, she came. She knew I'd developed a love/hate relationship with work. It was becoming increasingly difficult for me to deal with the system and the 24-hour shifts. Now her words assuaged me; she knew the world of emotions, feelings and compassion, and she knew the world of nurturing, for she was a nurse as well as a mother and my wife.

More tears and anguish flowed from me. "Can't they see what's happening?" I demanded. "Can't they understand my responsibility for the little girl's injury?"

"Maybe we should go outside," Janis said. I nodded, and we walked through the door that led to the bank of the millpond right outside the ER call room window, into which the Crystal River flowed with its cool, clear waters.

I sat down on the warm, brown grass at the base of a pine tree that supported my tired back. In a while, Fran brought out some hot tea for me.

My hand now moved gently over the grass, touching the tips of the new green growth just starting to emerge through the brown blanket that had covered and protected the earth during the winter months.

Swallows, free of worry, flew over the pond.

The water reflected the trees, clouds and sun.

A breeze made its invisible presence known by touching the center of the pond, creating a ripple amidst the mirrored images, breaking the illusion of sameness between sky and water, replacing it with dancing lights.

"Are you all right?" Fran asked.

"Just need a little more time," I muttered. Then I'd be ready to go back to the ER. "I just need a little longer to sit and talk about life, about how strange it is and how quickly it changes."

Another 30-40 minutes went by, and Fran returned.

"I'm feeling fine," I replied before he could ask. I would complete my shift, I thought.

The staff thought otherwise and contacted another physician to come in and replace me.

I protested, but it didn't help. Fran grabbed my hand and firmly said, "We called Jim, and he's coming in."

That one of my colleagues who lived over 30 miles away would drop everything and be willing to come in on a Sunday stunned me. Now I'd broken an unwritten rule: do not leave your post except under the direst of circumstances, such as significant illness or family tragedy. This was neither; this was one of those "emotional problems."

Another part of me knew it would be impossible for me to walk back in to the ER. A couple of hours passed, and finally, it was time to go home. I left, a leader who'd failed, left his command, a warrior who'd lost the battle.

Walking around in the quietness of our home, my mind seemed blank except for my occasional futile attempts to grasp what had happened or wrestle with feelings of immense concern and guilt over Shauna Lee's fate. And what of her parents and the agony they must be feeling?

How ingrained my fear of failure and avoidance of feelings had become. How heavy my own judgment of myself had become. A shroud of silence covered the rest of the day.

The second day also went slowly. The house was painfully quiet—no phone calls. No word came from the trauma center. I couldn't call, fearing the news. No news was good news— perhaps Shauna Lee had fallen in to a permanent coma—perhaps that would be best.

Early on the morning of the third day, the phone rang.

Is this the call? Am I ready to handle the tragedy it will hold?

I'd had time to prepare; I knew, as a physician, that "these things happen all the time."

I picked up the phone. The trauma center's nurse said, "Doctor Burgstede?"

As she continued, a prayerful stillness came over me. Shauna Lee had been put on a respirator to keep her body completely still, to give her a chance to recover as much brain function as possible.

The time had arrived to find out what would become of Shauna Lee when the paralyzing agent and the sedating agents were removed from her body and the respirator stopped, and she awoke...

A moment later I was listening in disbelief to the nurse's words.

"What did you say?" I asked. What she was saying couldn't be real, what I heard just wasn't possible... or they must have confused Shauna Lee with another patient.

But the nurse's voice said again, "Doctor Burgstede, Shauna Lee is fine; in fact, we believe, she'll have no residual damage from her injury."

No, it wasn't possible, not possible at all. I knew what had happened; I knew what I'd seen and yet...

Suddenly I was hit by an arrow. An arrow that pierced right through my armor. An arrow that directly hit the center of my heart. An arrow that made my chest ache with profound beauty.

Sorrow instantly became joy. *Things are going to be all right!*

I held the phone's mouthpiece away from my face. "Shauna Lee made it!" I yelled. "She made it," I said again, softer, nodding in disbelief.

"Yes, yes, she made it," the nurse repeated.

I hung up the phone, and tears flowed freely.

Joy shook me, and my beliefs of what was possible had been shattered. *The impossible had happened.*

An inner calmness returned during the next hour and I knew I could return to my duties and my normal life as Dr. Gil.

Later that week, on Easter Sunday, I was ready for Dave's funeral. I left my white armor at home, resting it for my next shift in the ER. Shauna Lee had opened a place inside me for my friend the heart surgeon who had died, who had tried so hard to find something, who had wrestled with the darkness, and who'd had to leave.

Invisible hopes and dreams of the heart are passed from one person to another on days like this. We all have a family that's not our physical family; we carry on for others who went as far as they could. We carry on for those who carried the vision and the dream of the heart's return. We're given the vision and dream of the heart's love as sacred gifts to hold, passed down since ancient times. Each time retelling the stories of healing, living the stories, completing the next phase of the vision of love manifesting, and then passing it on as a gift to those who are preparing and waiting for us to release it.

The service officially marked the end of Dave's physical life and went quickly with words from family and friends that gifted us. For me it came as an inner reassurance of our lives' eternal nature as a strand in the endless story and tapestry of life.

Those leaving the sanctuary made distant chatter as they filed past pictures of Dave before returning to their lives. Pictures, memories and ashes were what would be left and forgotten, it seemed.

Now the sanctuary emptied, but for a fatherless daughter and son talking quietly to someone near the pulpit.

I stood alone in the middle of the sanctuary, my heart overflowing, as a recorded song called, The Temple of the Heart, by Sophia[1], filled the air:

...peace is now reigning in the temple of the heart, in my heart, in my heart, in the temple of my heart.

The pathos of our life's journey mixed with the sweet fragrance of hundreds of lilies that were scattered throughout the periphery of the sanctuary. The Easter promise of the return of the heart revealed itself again as the words from Sophia's song continued filling me:

...Love is now reigning...Beauty is now reigning...

Lilies, whose white trumpets call warriors home to the healing fields...

Wisdom is now reigning...Strength is now reigning...Joy is now reigning...

I felt the temple of the heart inside and out, so beautiful and timeless—its love eternal. The words faded as I stepped deeper into the moment, into the peace beyond all understanding:

Peace is now reigning in the temple of my heart, in my heart,
in my heart,
in the temple of my heart.

Peace to you David, dear friend and fellow physician. Peace to you.

The encounter with Shauna Lee proved a defining moment in my life. As the weeks passed, I felt the connection to my heart center grow ever deeper. The daily doses of "healing energy" coming from focused inner awareness on my heart began renewing me as the intensity of my mind's outer search for answers lessened. I was awakening, becoming conscious,

---

[1] *Lyrics to 'The Temple of the Heart" are used with the express permission of Sophia.*

becoming aware of my thoughts, watching them and also experiencing gratitude that there was such a mystery to participate in.

Every morning, while it was still dark, I lit a small candle in the corner of Janis' and my bedroom. I kneeled, my eyes closed. My hands moved slowly and with great care to come and rest gently over my heart center, and I felt the wonder of warmth and light in the center of my chest. Centered, daily, something was being fed and growing... just beyond my understanding. My heart now came first, every day.

My journey to the heart center was now evidenced in my separation from the familiar everyday routines and the institution and city that had been my stable home for 15 years.

And the unexplainable yearning to follow my heart and heal myself deepened.

The encounter with Shauna Lee had shown me that engaging feelings was crucial to health and couldn't be ignored forever, lest feelings erupt uncontrollably, as they had for me, or if unexpressed in some way, fester as a dis-ease or dis-order. I now understood how immense anger or anguish could explode from someone who'd been "well-controlled, pleasant and safely armored" his or her whole life. How many living time bombs were out there? When and how could they be disarmed safely with the power of the heart?

I would learn and be taught again and again through further encounters in the ER, when, with my awareness anchored in my heart center, I could feel compassion and be with another's struggles, yet not be swept away by my own feelings or the feelings he or she might need to express to help his or her own healing.

Was it the revelation of the heart center's unifying energy that was the healing gift under all anger and anguish? Was a filled heart the answer to all emptiness?

Thinking and feeling were being subsumed from time to time by a new way of being with life—from the heart center's perspective. Life was now a journey to more and more engage the energies of unity, balance and healing that came from within.

I couldn't articulate it, but it was happening to me again and again. Life's suffering and despair had meaning; they were bringing me to the well of the center of who and what I was over and over. In those difficult times of great despair in the ER, the heart center's attributes of unconditional love, a healing presence, innate harmony and compassion were experienced more and more.

I would also again use healing circles to create healing fields. How natural this seemed in times of healing crises, bringing us all together—physician, patient and family—turning on our hearts, turning us all in to healers, all fully present to the moments at hand. I would sense and feel that energy again and again in the years to come, within men's groups and the opening circle of gatherings with healthcare professionals. I would sense it in my hands as a current flowing from one hand to the other through the circle. Circles as geometric forms inherently engage the energy we all share equally as a vital part of life—and every link was needed, for we were all healers seeking our wholeness.

People involved would confide in me: "My hands felt different when I reached out and held another's hand." And I'd smile at them and say, "Yes, I know."

It was a time to write and record the inward journey to the heart center and how it related to my outer world, to continue exploring other realms of healing—the inner world of dreams and healing images, inner dynamics and Jungian psychology. It was a time to deepen my understanding of healing and how people can come together to shift from the ordinary self to the healer self and engage the energies of a healing presence and change reality. It was a time to realize that people feel and experience touch (and connection) differently—touch can be an unconscious physical act (nurture or sex), or a mental (discipline and control) outwardly oriented and clinical act, or it can come from our center and be a deep, unifying, expansive and life-fulfilling act.

Life was changing again and a year later, it was time for me to leave for another ER. There I would work six to seven 24-

hour shifts a month, hoping to find even more time to explore healing and the experience of wholeness in more ways.

Yet crisis again would be the real teacher.

6
The Red Truck

And a child will lead us.

It was two o'clock in the morning of my first call day in the new ER. This being an unfamiliar place, I was concerned about how the nursing staff would receive me.

Reggie, the night nurse, was a full-bodied woman—a veteran who'd worked the graveyard shift for over ten years and had broken in many physicians. She let me know right away, "I'm not married, was once, but the guy was a bum. Best thing I ever did was get rid of him." Yes, she was in charge, this was her territory. A twinkle in her eye suggested that my attentive ear had caught her approval.

The ambulance sirens announced the patient's arrival. Erv was a big man, well over 300 lb., and he had so much fluid in his body from chronic heart failure, it gave him a bloated appearance, as if he'd been stuffed into his striped blue-and-white Oshkosh B' Gosh bib overalls and white t-shirt. His neck was so thick, he was hardly able to turn; his crew cut and attire marked him as a no-nonsense farmer.

Reggie knew Erv and his family; she now rattled off the names of relatives scattered about the surrounding landscape of the town, as well as some of their medical problems. The nursing assistant Jodie nodded back and added a juicy tidbit Reggie hadn't known. "Oh?" Reggie replied, as if a bit surprised there was something she wasn't aware of.

Then Reggie said loudly and matter-of-factly: "When it's your time, it's your time. If I ever come in that condition, you leave me alone." Her stern voice, coupled with a wagging index finger, made sure the warning was intense enough, as if she thought I might forget if I happened to be the one on duty when she came in.

Erv was suffering from depression, severe heart failure, irregular heartbeat and severe heart valve problems. Indeed, I sensed Reggie was right: it was his last stand. The situation was grim; the possibility of meaningful recovery simply didn't exist. The patient showed great courage and acceptance and indicated to me that he no longer wanted intervention, motioning a "No" with his head and his hand to offers to do this or that to prolong his life. He was very tired and ready to die.

This was the first time since Shauna Lee that I would extend an invitation to create a circle, this time around the bed, for loved ones to share last words. But now I felt different—centered and natural. The fire of past experience had matured me, and now I was firmly grounded with my awareness in my heart center. Feelings weren't overwhelming me, nor were my thoughts conflicted about what to do, or if creating the circle was right for the situation.

Families often came in with conflicts and fears about death, with religious differences, or with unspoken wounds and separations that precluded such a gathering. There are times for everything, and I sensed this was a time for a healing circle. Other times, what's needed is something like individual quiet time with the patient or time with the family pastor or hospital chaplain. But this crisis had arrived suddenly, and the patient was still lucid, still able to interact with us, even though his heart was now beating so irregularly, I knew death could occur at any moment.

My body began to relax, my mind quieted and my heart opened.

I said, "Let's join hands and make a circle." The words came naturally, warmly, and the heart's invitation deepened quickly. One hand reached out for another, linking one body to another, creating a temple of hearts for an ailing heart, and a song of hearts, all of us tuning in to the same frequencies of unity and healing.

The circle formed, and this act alone invited the light and awareness of the heart's power to enter. Eight of us held the heavy breaths of a tired man. I said only a few words about being present and honoring the moment and allowing our awareness to rest in our hearts, and then silence deepened the experience. Hearts were invited to remain open to the act of honoring and being present to the impending death as fully as we could. Then, stepping back, we released our hands, and the circle enlarged.

I said, "Would anyone like to step into the circle and say something?" My heart's voice calmed the uncertainty of the others, who'd never been in a place like this before, so intimately involved in death as they prepared to witness the last breath.

No one moved in toward the center, toward the dying heart, and slowly, the hesitancy to interact became painful. The adults looked away from me or toward the ground. Even Erv's wife was unsure, perhaps afraid of public tears.

Just to my left I felt the resistance of the silent older son, Matt, who was zipped up tightly in his heavy black leather jacket. I sensed he stood struggling with the ancient barrier between a father and a son, powerful, invisible, remaining even in the face of death—a "tradition" inscribed with these words: "No tears are to be shed, no feelings felt; you are a strong man, you are a warrior."

In the circle stood two young, crew cut grandsons, both dark-haired, the youngest about four, the other about seven. I saw no uncertainty in their eyes, for they'd clearly not yet learned to fear this transition. They didn't see it or know it as "the end" that we adults perceive death to be.

The patient was so large and tired; it was difficult for him to move his head sideways. He was focused only on breathing and fighting death, as well as releasing and opening to it, so he was unable to give much attention to his family.

Again I extended the invitation: "Is there anything anyone would like to say?"

Silence followed. But I knew that inner heroes, who come as healers, are sometimes born at times like this—inner heroes who can go where ordinary outer heroes cannot, and break through barriers that paralyze others with fear. My heart called out for such a healer, such a champion of the heart, who didn't fear death-defying love.

For some reason all eyes turned to the youngest boy in his new blue-bib overalls. Perhaps we sensed he was the fearless one. Perhaps we discerned that he had the courage, the heart and the capacity to step through where we couldn't.

His smile then radiated joy, and he stepped into the circle, though perhaps not knowing he had the golden presence, and hands that could touch unconditionally, that could go where no adult hands could yet go. He looked at us all, as if for direction. We, of course, didn't know what to do but smile back at him. Yet I knew the inner hero, the healer, had come, though innocent and naïve of his power.

His eyes twinkled at his grandpa, and he asked, "Do you remember that red truck you gave me?" My throat tightened; my ears strained to hear. All of us awaited the dying man's reply, as if the world's most important question had just been asked—the only question that really mattered.

"Yes," Erv nodded. The boy's little hand reached out to touch Erv's left hand. It was a touch so profound and so gentle and so powerful that it awakened us all. Erv's struggling face began its change with the appearance of a faint smile, and a sweetness spread that transformed him. His head turned as his old, rough, weary hands enfolded his grandson's hand for a last eternal moment. Tender and innocent, the boy's touch thus released the energy of love throughout the room. My now warm chest confirmed it.

Now, no barrier could hold the love back, nor did we resist its entry. The little boy rocked his body slightly from side to side and looked at us all so proudly, as if to say, "See. It's not so hard." A few gentle laughs arose from the circle, followed by joyful tears because such a great young hero had appeared in our midst.

Then the older, taller grandson stepped into the circle, moved to his grandpa's left side, near his heart, and rested his small, dark head for a moment on his grandpa's dying heart. Next he placed his ear close to his grandfather's lips, listening for the whispered message of love. Now he moved back into the circle, to wait for other inner heroes and heroines to be born in those precious moments, which now called more urgently and more deeply as physical death drew closer and would soon close the door to love.

No longer constrained by old patterns of behavior, roles, guilt or shame, no longer afraid to heal or of death, one by one, the others from the circle stepped in to say their last words. Erv's wife and then the other adults followed, lending their own healing energy. Some spoke aloud. Some whispered into the old man's ear, their whispers carrying messages of love from the deepest parts of their hearts into the deepest recesses of the heart of the dying man. Kisses moved intimately through the ear canal, and then echoed through Erv's mind and entire body.

Finally, only Matt was left. He was dark-haired, like the little boys, and he was standing alone. His protective black leather jacket was now open, revealing a slit of white between the two sides of the heavy metal zipper. Only a thin layer of cotton now remained to cover his heart.

We all waited, holding this last space for him. A quick glance in his direction revealed to me the ancient, powerful forces still struggling within him "to be what a man was supposed to be"— to be what men had so highly esteemed for generations—strong in the face of adversity, remaining in the mind, never collapsing into feelings or tears, defending what's been and is, revealing no vulnerability, being a man of power, a warrior, denying death its healing moment.

His vow to be true to a man's way was invisible, yet I felt it powerfully. His mind struggled to control his body, and even resist the heart, as other powerful internal forces called to him desperately, as if this might be the last opportunity in his life when he might let go and step through the barrier. But the door was now unlocked; it was time to heal, to release the inner turmoil of separation so obviously tormenting him. His own wound of separation was calling: a sacred wound, a divine wound.

No one could do anything for him; only he could decide. The Temple of the Heart, that place within that holds unconditional love, waited for his complete surrender; nothing less would be enough. We waited for the moment when its beauty would become overwhelming and no longer resistible. We waited for death to allow birth...

We waited...

The inner heroes who come to heal are born moment by moment. The deepest chambers of the heart wait for weary warriors to release their armor needed for the outer battles of life—armor that precludes them from entering the healing fields. The inner hero, who is the healer and champion of the heart waits patiently, as it has throughout all generations before, for its time. The children of the world wait patiently—the women, the old men—all wait patiently, as, in the tension of stillness, we in that room now waited.

And then the moment came. With a final deep breath, he called on all the courage he could find, stepped into the circle and moved to his father's right side. Then quickly coming down, chest pressing against chest. Left cheek pressing against left cheek, Matt disappeared into the blackness of his coat that pulled itself over his head, covering and protecting him during the long-awaited and feared embrace that pulled him inwardly to home. Now the wail of long held love erupted from the depths of the young man's heart. Now they wept together deeply in the Temple of the Heart, their tears coming to wash away the pain of separation, to lighten the armor, allowing Matt to feel his own heroic self as a healer and feel the heroism and healing of his father.

Hearts throughout the room wept deeply in that moment; all hearts must weep when it comes.

Life had come to bless his son. His father's work now done, the great gift given and shared, Erv began lapsing into unconsciousness, as the experience of internal and eternal peace imbued the room.

***

I was profoundly moved by the expressions of love in that circle, of the sense of healing energy that permeated the room, and the deep energies of healing that coursed through my body every time I remembered and felt the image of father and son uniting in the center of the circle.

Could it be that the era of great conflict was beginning to end?

Battles for thousands of years both internal and external done?

The last weary warriors coming home?

That in the ashes of the great circle of death,
*   champions of the heart can now arise?*

Joy streaming down cheeks cleansing our armor?

I wondered was it time.

I wondered: Could such great healing and unity only occur near the time of physical death? Could only that be the time when the healing fields could appear, the only time when humans could end the disconnection from their hearts and shift and liberate the heart's energies? Was it the only time a parent and child could embrace that differently, deeply and expansively, and experience the radiance of wholeness that ensued?

I would see again and again, in near death experiences and with actual physical death, that immense love was often released because hearts were opened. Those expressions of grace, the healing and unifying events, were never predictable. Yet I knew we were being given some glimpses of how love worked, an expanding understanding—a tool (focusing on our center) and the capacity together to create the field of unifying energy where healing and wholeness might happen.

New eyes were often given to see crisis and death differently, even benevolently, as a transition time to deeper and more expansive experiences of the heart's unifying energies. As an internal and eternal peace liberated, in a singular moment for all who embraced the event, to release pain and sorrow and suffering and experience the radiance of wholeness.

I continued to record these stories and the wondrous healing images that went with them. Occasionally I was blessed with someone sharing their dreams about the radiance of individuals who had passed. They were universal images of wholeness and radiance (liberated love) that were healing and gave comfort when expressed and deeply received. Did they speak of the reality we can all experience at times other than just before physical death?

A shift began with increased focus on the struggles of others who were challenged by death, by being alone and in more difficult ways.

Perhaps it was the most confusing and greatest of crises I would witness. It was a mystery no one seemed to be able to solve. It was an act over ten million people are estimated to contemplate every year and over one million attempt and over 40,000 succeed at.

7

Will Anyone Understand?

Death reminds us of what is important.

"We found him this way," the ambulance crewmember said. "He was lying in his bed, snoring heavily, and we were unable to wake him up."

They were very familiar with Alan. All told, this was his eleventh documented attempt to commit suicide, and the attempts were continually getting more serious. This time they'd found an open container of antifreeze in the garage.

The nurse told me about everything the family had been through over the years—guilt, grief, anger, helplessness, and finally, exhaustion and apathy. It had been going on for nearly ten years, and Alan was now in his late 20s.

The family wouldn't be coming in this time; they lived far away. They'd been called, but they just couldn't do it one more time. They understood there was nothing we could do to save him. They didn't want anything else done; they wanted comfort only. Could he be transferred closer to them, they wondered?

I walked into his room, a quiet one in the corner of the ER. I saw a lean young man with short red hair, whose body was covered with a white sheet and blanket. He snored heavily, between long stretches of apnea (times when his breath would stop for up to half a minute or so).

Alan's skin was pasty, and from the look of things, he'd been like this for a day or two. He made no movement or response to my rubbing his chest with my knuckle, a usually painful test that would awaken even the most intoxicated patient. His eyes were glassy, fixed, and stared right through me, indicating that his mind was no longer functioning.

I bent over and listened to his lungs and the sounds of secretions building up. The lungs were breathing irregularly, as if giving up, perhaps too tired to support his life of suffering any longer.

I listened to his heart; the beat was still so regular, so present, still beating on.

He made no more purposeful physical actions. Only the heart throbbed on, *lub-dub, lub-dub, lub-dub.*

Indeed, nothing could be done to save him. Due to severe failure of the liver and kidneys caused by the antifreeze, his body and mind had been destroyed.

I told the nurse in attendance, "We can't do anything this time."

I found a certain peace coming with those words uttered out of a sense of compassion for his struggle. He'd been trying his best, I sensed, but he'd been on the edge of darkness for so long, he'd finally given up hope.

The lights in the room had been dimmed. Now the only movement and sound in the room came from my breath, his breath and the heart monitor, that showed his heart continuing to work as it sometimes does even when a mind and body are totally gone. I watched the monitor and wondered about his heart and his life. Was there, or would there be, a moment of redemption for him? Was there some purpose in his death?

Beep, Beep, Beep...

Deep inside his chest and in his heart, that organ's natural pacemaker continued to work. A small group of cells generated a powerful pulse of electromagnetic energy every second or so that went through the whole heart, a signal every cell waited for, to contract and keep the heart going, all working together for the whole, everything depending on that signal and the responses to it. The organ that gave and received, gave and received, gave and received endlessly, unconditionally, to the whole body, powered by that pulse, that energetic beat, that burst of light on the inside.

Electrodes dotted his chest, now picking up the invisible pulses of electrical energy at the surface of the skin and transmitting these to the monitor, where they could be seen. The invisible electromagnetic pulse that actually moved out to touch every cell of the body and then out to fill the room (scientifically, already recorded over ten feet away), was now visible, the silent, now given a voice: *Beep, beep, beep...*

The drive to breathe was still there, but it was weakening, becoming more erratic. His tongue was now falling backwards, obstructing the breath. To help ease his transition, I placed a small curved tube in his mouth to keep his tongue up.

Now his breath settled down, and I watched again and waited, listening to his breath and heart. The nurse left, but I stayed. It seemed important to me that one of us be there. No one should die alone.

I stood in silence, my eyes fixed on the monitor, drawn into the image and sounds of the heartbeat, ears fixed on its sounds. I realized that his heart was beginning to teach me something beyond my mind, and I surrendered to the moment.

Beep, beep, beep, beep, beep, beep, beep, beep, beep, beep: the green waves and spikes of the heart's pulse marched along on the monitor's screen.

Standing alone, I watched the pulse and listened, now feeling into his life, his birth into this world and what it was like, his yearning, his battles and struggles, his sacrifice.

Beep, beep, beep...

Now my awareness strangely shifted inward, and an image of a flat, gray granite gravestone appeared. Partially covered by surrounding grass and brown fall leaves. A gust of wind blew away the leaves, revealing Alan's name. I stared at the stone and his name and felt transported into that future. Did anyone understand why he had to die? Or what was at the heart of this mystery of his yearning for death?

I could see the cold fall wind blowing through the cemetery. It was a place to contemplate death—filled with old tombstones, most crooked, many whose granite was worn, the names erased by time, standing under ancient oak trees. New flat gravestones were there, too, and new young trees stood near his grave in the newer section of the cemetery.

In my vision, I stared at the stone—the only reminder left of him—this gray stone with his name on it...

Then the image faded, and the room returned.

Beep, beep, beep...

Would anyone understand what he'd been searching for?

Beep, beep, beep...
Would anyone understand why he'd had to suffer so?
Beep, beep, beep...
Would anyone understand why he had to die?
Beep..., beep.........
For days afterward, the images and feeling of his struggles stayed with me, and I asked over and over: *Why?*

I wouldn't forget. I couldn't forget. I *needed* to know why. He would be remembered, his struggles would be remembered, his heartbeat would be remembered; they would live on. In my journal I drew the image of his gravestone, and by it I placed the words: *Do not forget.*

In many ways I was now beginning to question the suffering and yearning of such individuals to die physical deaths, rather than die to the old reality of life and beliefs they were living. What was this difference? And how could we in medicine address this difference?

Could we find some way to erase or release the old programs and fixed beliefs in the mind that seemed to cause such pain and self-judgment? Could we stop the "same old, same old" hurting scripts and images?

The healing journey continued. Another teacher with a profoundly beautiful lesson was coming to help me understand the inner dynamics involved in our lives and to show me yet another way to find what it is we seek. She was a teacher who would reveal the core of healing, the light of healing, the power we are all trying to die for and awaken to.

8

Rose's Heart

*When the moment of healing comes,
a lifetime of suffering is transformed by a radiance of love.*

The flashing red lights and wailing sirens of the ambulance began and then faded as it moved out into the night.

It was Saturday, and I was alone, fatigued, surrounded by darkness and the silence of my hospital call room, drifting off to familiar thoughts, surfing the channels of my mind, searching for more answers to life's challenges. Slowly the incessant inner chatter faded, and my head released to the soft pillow. But the peace it held lasted only briefly.

Ring, ring, ring. The phone startled me for a moment, and then the reality of the room quickly returned.

The nurse said, "*She's* here again, and in heart failure."

"I'm on my way," I replied, not asking who "she" was, instinctively reaching out through the darkness to touch the white coat draped over the familiar orange vinyl chair at the foot of the call bed. It slipped on and eased me, like an old trusted friend might.

I stepped out into the hall, where two dim red lights revealed exits from the dark deserted section of the hospital where my call room was located. My shadow entered the empty rooms, while I moved toward the stairwell. A familiar pattern of thinking recurred as my fingers closed the buttons on my white coat and my eyes adjusted to the dim lights: *Twenty years in medicine, and so much has changed, and yet, in other ways, it seems as if nothing's changed.* In some ways, my work had become routine and almost always predictable. A brief shudder of resignation passed through me as I slipped the last button securely into place.

At the bottom of the stairwell, the door opened into another darkened corridor, which led directly to the ER. Straightening my back, I quickened my pace, my posture assuming the natural and expected doctor's confidence.

I'd follow the familiar proven ways expected for this type of crisis—a protocol: gather information from the nurse, discuss the history and concerns with the patient and the family, then do a physical examination, an electrocardiogram, laboratory and x-ray studies, and then decide on a final plan of action.

My awareness was already in the ER, sensing what wanted to be revealed, anticipating the first visual contact, the almost immediate knowledge of prognosis, and the next action required. I'd always follow this plan, except under those direst circumstances, which demanded immediate intervention.

Heart failure had uncertainties, but only two outcomes: life or death—or so I thought.

If our efforts were successful, in a few hours the patient would show some improvement and possibly be brought back to her original condition by the following day. I loved this scenario; it was so dramatic, so miraculous.

But what if a different sequence unfolded? An arrest—needing CPR, or even a respirator? Or, if failure and death ensued?

A forbidden and never-shared thought came, one that if I voiced it would betray the image of the caring doctor I'd cultivated over so many years: *No complications, please.*

I hoped for no inconveniences that would disrupt the flow of the ER and disrupt the tidiness and orderliness of the night. That evening, I wanted nothing to interfere with the few hours of rest or sleep my body needed so much. And above all, let there be no deaths!

I thought positively, *Yes, tonight there will be success and life and a quick return to the normal routine. It will be a good night.*

The Emergency Room doors swung open automatically with a touch of the metal bar. Bright, harsh fluorescent lights forced my eyes to squint. After only a few more steps in the short hallway, my secret thoughts went back in to hiding.

Turning to the right, my eyes were greeted by a pile of medical records stacked almost a foot high on the counter in front of the nursing station. The nurse nodded and her expression changed slightly, transmitting all of her concerns instantly and silently.

"Failure five times this year," she said. Indeed, the nurse and the ambulance crew knew Rose and her problems well. One glance at the last face sheet on the pile attested to her close calls with death, multiple episodes of congestive heart failure and two heart attacks, in addition to a host of other medical conditions that together portrayed a very difficult life. Hundreds upon hundreds of pages described in detail her physical ordeals with her weakened heart, but I had no time to go through the records.

The nurse summarized, "She's had increasing shortness of breath this week, more swelling in her legs, and now she's becoming anxious and confused."

The double doors of Trauma Room Number One opened inwardly, revealing a cream-colored room of about 20 square feet, bathed in soft light. The latest equipment stood around its periphery like sentinels.

Through the doorway, I could see a woman of average build in her late 70s on the examination bed. She sat upright, only a loose, white, blue-speckled ER gown covering her aged body. Her short, straight, wispy gray hair was unkempt, and a little clump stuck straight out just above her right ear, as unruly as the intrusion of this crisis. Near her on her left side stood a husband, daughter and son, who'd just arrived and been brought into the room by the ward clerk to support her in her struggle to breathe and live.

Looking up, she labored and struggled for every breath. A woman of the land and elements, her skin was pale and weathered, and an image came to me, perhaps from her past: She was sitting on a tractor on a hot sunny day, pulling a baler and a hay wagon.

Silently, she exuded something else that moved me—dignity.

Her breath rattled through the watery foam in her bronchi and trachea—this rattle becomes louder and louder just before death in heart failure patients. Deep, long breaths forced her to look upward, her eyes opening wider, her rib muscles pulling her chest outward as she sucked in air. She prolonged her in-and-out breaths as she fought to get air to move through the foam and water. Each breath was precious to her. Nothing else mattered; in truth, all she had left was breath.

She glanced toward me, grinning nervously, as if sharing an intimate secret—of death—that only the two of us understood.

Death was in the room with her, whispering louder and louder with each raspy breath, beginning to surround her. The anxiety created by the whispering of death was filling her body.

She was prepared for her emergency. An IV was already in her left hand, a nasal cannula was giving her oxygen, and monitors were watching her pulse and recording her blood pressure and oxygen levels.

The nurse proceeded through the door ahead of me. I followed, but then, strangely, my usual sense of assuredness and confidence began to disappear. Hesitating, I stopped just outside the doorway, sensing that something very unexpected was about to happen.

A voice came from within me, as if some inner wisdom was talking: *You will not do what you've always done. You'll walk in and sit at her right side and touch her right forearm with your hand. Then, in silence, connect your heart to hers, through your hand, through your eyes and through your presence.*

A sudden knowingness, a deep familiarity, settled into me. It began as a faint feeling in my chest. Remembering the inward path, my awareness moved to follow it; I felt my breath and my body relaxing. Then my awareness moved into the center of my chest—my heart center—and I stepped through the open doorway. I knew I was not going to do what I'd always done.

The nurse looked up from behind the raised head of the bed. "Do we need any medication?" she questioned. In silence, I motioned, "no." And in a way that conveyed understanding, I watched her quietly step out of the room.

On the opposite side of the bed, Rose's husband, Arden, stood anxiously at arm's length, breathing with his wife, connecting with her, breathing the difficult labored breaths with her and for her.

Mary, her daughter, a tall woman in her late 40s, was standing to his right. With her light complexion and long blond hair, she seemed so different from her mother, and yet her eyes and body spoke of a deep closeness between them.

Ron, the son, younger and slightly shorter than the daughter, had darker skin and short dark hair. He seemed perplexed, but present nonetheless. Here were the three most important people in her life. With my presence, we were four hearts surrounding the failing one.

We all engaged the crisis in silence. No words came. Stillness reigned; presence was full and undivided. We were no longer physician, family members, or patient, but participants and witnesses. Five beings connected to their hearts.

The guardrail of the bed on my side was folded out horizontally, as if to provide a small platform. Her right arm lay there, her palm down, waiting.

My awareness moved deep inside again, connecting to my breath —breath, soft and full, belly soft, expanding with the breath. A deep calm flowing downward through my body, releasing all tension. Connecting deeper and deeper into my core, manifesting: a natural silence, a calm, a peace beyond understanding. Warmth came to the center of my chest; my "white armor" becoming transparent and then opening. The fullness of energy expanding outward, beyond skin, carrying awareness that radiated softly in all directions, like a spherical mist of light from a candle. From Rose, I sensed the same subtle kind of presence coming toward me, and we tuned in together.

My right hand, which had always probed clinically for answers under such conditions and under the direction of the mind, released itself. Through my eyes, love and gratitude flowed to that hand. It moved toward her forearm with its own wisdom, as if called to that exact destination at just the right time and in just the right way, as if it had been waiting with an innate reverence for a long, long time, just for this moment.

My fingers first moved through a subtle layer of energy, so easily felt, just above her skin, and then came to rest, with a touch as light and powerful as grace itself. Grace gently touching her forearm about three inches above her wrist. Watching and feeling my hand in a new and different way—so natural and soft resting on her skin—merging in oneness, making my hand feel strangely and wonderfully different. Awareness now rested deeply within both of us, as we were pulled inward.

Eyes met eyes, left eye gazed gently into left eye, clear windows into expanding darkness and emptiness. A recognition occurred then; faint smiles developed, going deeper and deeper, remembering...

The room, the lights, the people, and the machines seemed to disappear. Who was the healer? Who was the heal*ee*? All thoughts, desires and agendas dissolved. All boundaries and distinctions gone, stillness and witnessing reigned. Her head turned upward and toward the left.

And then it came. Her eyes and yearning body greeted its revelation and then turning slowly back and straight ahead as if looking out through the doors of the room.

Her eyelids filled, welling up with tears. Reflections of a rainbow appeared there, tiny gem-like dancers, all in a row, dancing joyously, leaping here, jumping there, a hint of green, a hint of blue, a hint of red, a hint of yellow—all sparkling like diamonds that grew in number and size, filling up her eyes completely, welling over, and then letting go.

First, her right eye released its joy, on a crooked path down the weathered skin of her cheek—long, glistening, like a river seen from far above on a sunny day. And then the left eye released its tears, flowing slowly to her weary body: flowing downward, dripping on the cloth below, soaking through and then touching parched flesh. Healing moisture making whole.

No hands stopped the flow or hid the joy. Her face wet, glowing and radiant, her body, now released of so much tension was filled with divine peace.

Her first words carried newfound strength and fullness. "I've had a good life," she said, her voice filled with gratitude and grace.

The moment had arrived. At death's door, she claimed the impossible.

All traces of fear were gone. Nothing need be undone; everything she'd experienced in life had served. She was free and filled with joy.

When the intensity of the moment faded, I asked, "Would you like to say anything else?"

"I am ready to go home," she said. I understood in that moment, home was the physical home and the "home experience" the fulfillment of her destiny. We smiled.

I turned and softly asked the family, "Do you understand what she said?" They nodded, yes.

Amazingly, her breath was now deep and strong. Her complexion ruddy, her body alive. She'd need no more IVs, ambulance runs, ER visits or hospitalizations.

Having been so gifted, and having gifted us completely, she left the hospital with her family. I left too, in the morning, grateful for another part of some mystery that had been revealed, of the peace that can be found in the midst of the most powerful storms of life.

As life would have it, two months later, I was standing at the ER entrance when Rose's daughter Mary, who was visiting a friend in the hospital, walked up to me. I could see she was carrying her mother's radiance with her.

She said, "You know my mother just passed away, don't you?"

"No, I hadn't heard," I replied.

"Not a day went by without her talking about what happened that night in the Emergency Room," she said.

We stood in silence, remembering the night that had brought us together, looking into each other with gentle ease. Then we embraced and began breathing together.

And at that moment, I felt something I never had before. It began as a sense of warmth developing between us, outside and yet between our chest walls, as if a third heart had appeared there. And I felt infused with the same sense of radiance I'd felt in Rose's presence, a radiant love, an awareness of unity that permeated my body and filled it like nothing else ever had.

Parting from the embrace, Mary and I acknowledged each other silently through our eyes. We'd been graced and nourished again in some way, beyond our ordinary comprehension.

The rest of that evening resonated with the new energies I carried from that encounter. My body and mind felt renewed and restored. Months later I would write these words in my journal:

When the moment of healing comes,
a lifetime of suffering is transformed by a radiance of
love.

I'd been deeply moved by what happened with Rose and then later with Mary and wanted to share what had happened with others.

I knew I wasn't alone in my yearning to heal and love more deeply and expansively. Somehow we had to find a place and space to leave the confines of our everyday lives and touch the depths of love—to leave and step through the doorway into that healing place where we can experience the peace beyond understanding.

So I began to share with others in various healthcare and healing professions what I'd learned about the energies of healing, holding a silent heart centered presence, and now about heart centered touch through the foundational process called heart centering...

9

Physician, Center Thyself!

A time for every purpose.
A time to heal (energetically center).

I developed a program to teach as a three-day conference for health care professionals. Janis was there too, presenting her own unique program for women on empowering their hearts, minds and bodies.

The program for physicians was directed toward engaging the heart of the healer. Physicians who came to the program wanted to explore what it means to restore and renew life through immersion in healing energies.

Twelve physicians, ten men and two women, who were entirely new to the process of heart centering, joined me to release the mental and physical intensities of our professional and personal lives. Together, we would step through a door into the once mysterious world of healing to practice the art and science of *energetic* healing.

The foundation of our program was the realization that everything is energetic in nature, and everything in the universe has a center. When we consciously connect our awareness to our "heart" center, which is the energetic center of our body's energy systems, we create a balancing and unifying experience—a healing presence. Like a teeter-totter, we can go up and down in our mentally created world, depressed or anxious (low-energy or high-energy), right or wrong, etc., which can also represent the opposites of thinking and feeling. Or, we can consciously connect to a third place, the fulcrum, where we find calm and balance. *Centering within,* we energetically experience precisely that calm and balanced power within ourselves.

The conferences addressed many questions and provided further information on how to begin to discover and energize the healer within. Some of the questions included:

-What is the difference between *healing* and *curing*?

-Why can the mind only cure (control, fix, cut out or remove certain symptoms), while only the heart can heal (restore balance to life and release symptoms caused by an imbalanced life)?

-Why is it essential to our health to be connected to our feelings?

-Why is touch such an integral part of healing?

-How can we discover and connect to a new form of touch that is healing?

-Why is it so difficult to release our addictions and our learned patterns of behavior that can be so destructive?

We began with a simple invitation—physically shake off the outside world and our identification with its reality, and then open to the heart's energetic field. Getting everyone to shake like a wet dog drying its coat is always so invigorating. This actual energetic process teaches us how to release the bound tension behind our everyday armor (and covering our center) quickly. When everyone does it together, it always leads to laughter and the shaking off of the dis-ease called "seriousness." It makes us lighter of heart.

After loosening up and laughing, we would sit down and begin discussing scientific studies on increasing longevity and quality of life by incorporating breathing techniques, caring presence, touch and deep communication with others into our practice.

We reviewed the two parts of the body's nervous system—the one that prepares us for fight or flight (called the sympathetic system), and the other one that brings calm to our bodies (called the parasympathetic system). The intensities of modern living often keep the sympathetic system turned on 24/7, flooding the body constantly with stress hormones such as adrenaline. Stress hormones become self-destructive, creating hypertension and microscopic tears in the arteries that then get patched with cholesterol. This hardening and thickening of the arteries causes many heart attacks and strokes. This excess of stress hormones "built up stress" is also one of the major underlying causes that contribute to a vast array of new physical and mental symptoms, and the many newly prescribed medications needed to control these symptoms. As the unbalanced life continues, we are mentally "wired" 24/7, and then physically burn out, living cycles of being stressed out and then burned out, with a resting place called zoned out.

How can we restore balance to such lives?

First, we explored the Eastern model of medicine. Based on the principles of living an "energetically balanced life," this model involves releasing blocks to the flow of life energy (also known as *chi and prana in the Eastern model and the life force and spirit in the Western model)* in the body. Then, we discussed the Eastern understandings of the body as an energy system, with energy centers and channels through which energy flowed from center to center. Eventually, by integrating these concepts, we would begin to realize how modern dis-ease and dis-order were created by living unbalanced lives that had lost touch with feelings and the body, as well as being disconnected from the center of our centers—the heart center.

Some simple experiential exercises were then introduced that let the physicians actually feel energy with their hands.

I said, "It's like the energy of heat; you can't see it, but you can feel it. Everything is energy. So, just relax, and get out of your mind. Let your body do the sensing, and it will come to you." Through the simple exercise of rubbing their hands together and placing their awareness on their hands, participants were able to begin sensing the energy field between their hands.

Next, we began to practice the art and science of shifting our awareness from the mind center to the heart center—a shift from the experience of thinking (which defines and separates on the outer level) to that of healing (unification within). We shifted from the outwardly oriented mind to the depth of the heart in order to create a relaxed and centered sense of self and allow connection to feelings without being overwhelmed by them.

Centering, it was explained, is experiencing the *inner* unity between thinking and feeling, the place of *energetic* healing that energetically returns balance to our lives. With centering, there is no need to fix, change or judge. Centering is the source and process for holding a silent, still, dynamically neutral, unifying presence for self and other. Dynamically neutral, yet powerful like a magnetic field. Just like the externally unifying experience of romantic love once was, but now as an internal unifying process that allows for profound unburdening, on the emotional, psychological, physical and mental levels. This unburdening of the symptoms associated with "an overwhelmed and overloaded outer life" can be profound. Seriousness is released, allowing lightheartedness to return as we awaken to the heart's power again.

We practiced this simple process of shifting several times until we could make the connections quickly—moving from awareness on thoughts in the mind to awareness on breath and the creation of a relaxed breath and body to awareness resting in the heart center. We practiced the art of transmitting and receiving this energy through hand-to-hand connection by holding hands and making a circle while simultaneously connecting our awareness to our hearts. Together we created a space that energetically supported inner and then outer unity on the personal and collective level—a living laboratory for empowerment, healing and insights.

Thereafter, many were startled by these new experiences and made observations such as these:

-"My mind only sees the surface of things, and I always react to any outer changes automatically."

-"I just realized *I* am not my *thoughts*; yet I can *watch* my thoughts."

-"I'm not my beliefs, I'm more than that."

-"I can't believe the tension I was always holding in my body—how tight my breathing was."

-"My hands feel different and wonderful."

We were waking up to a different way of engaging life.

The conversations then turned toward deep sharing, insight and laughter. Freeing old burdens creates a light heart. The power came and the courage came to speak and listen from the heart center.

We were seasoned medical warriors, and Frank, the white-haired elder of our group, began the sharing, "I've been in practice for fifty years. I do rounds every day and have a clinic on Saturdays, too."

Yes, he wants us to remember what real commitment is. He's the real thing.

Frank smiled.

Indeed, he'd earned his white hair and the dignity it carried.

His smile then slowly began to fade, as he revealed more. Tiredness and weariness began to be heard in his voice. He paused, and then he expressed that there was no one to take his place, that he was only one of a few doctors in his small rural town, and that this was a rare weekend away from his practice. He voiced the silent unspoken code: to always be there, to agree to never leave your post. He revealed the side of Dr. Bill I hadn't known when I started medicine. I reflected on my own life in medicine and the lack of a place to gather with others to share and reveal our deeper truths and yearnings and healing capacities.

More stories followed—of triumphs and struggles, of large successful practices and feelings of emptiness, of divorces, of family deaths. Frank was listening carefully, taking it in, shaking his head along with the stories.

There was nothing to fix; the heart of our circle could hold it all. We were there to witness, through the eyes and presence of the heart, our individual journeys to healing—each so unique and yet so similar to others. And we all acknowledged something that was hard to grasp beneath it all, something that had almost been forgotten—that inner desire and commitment that had brought us to medicine in the first place—to *heal.*

As another physician was talking to the group, Frank turned slowly and looked at me. I smiled, nodding my head, feeling and acknowledging who he was, the epitome of the devoted physician with his white-haired crown of wisdom. He smiled back, and then we returned our attention to the circle.

That evening Janis and I were passing by the large center hall of the conference complex. To our surprise, a big band celebration was in progress that same weekend. Elegance was in the air; tables were draped with elaborate ivory cloth and set with large silver candelabras of eight candles each and bottles of champagne and long-stemmed glasses; dessert china that held the remains of various chocolate delights were still on the tables.

The expansive dance floor was filled with men in black tuxedos and women in flowing gowns, all dancing slowly together around the room.

In the middle of all of this were two young lovers, spinning and dipping and gliding, their radiance filling the room. They weren't dressed like the others, though. The man was wearing a camel-colored sports jacket and brown slacks, and the brunette woman wore a white blouse and red skirt. They saw us and began dancing our way. Right in front of us, they treated us to a final dip. Perspiration dripped from the woman's forehead; she tried to catch her breath, fanning her face and neck with her right hand to cool herself down. Still out of breath, face flushed, her husband grinning boyishly, she beamed joyfully, sighing, "We haven't felt this way since our honeymoon!"

The couple was Frank and his wife of 50 years.

She said, "Tomorrow after the conference, we're calling all the children—we're going to have a reunion!" They laughed with each other, smiled at us and then re-entered the flow of dancers—he was lost in the ecstasy of the moment, and she occasionally looked over his shoulder to smile at us.

The next morning our group was ready for a session on heart centered touch. The lights dimmed, and the darkness settled in. The three exit signs were now the room's major sources of light. The doors were closed. Taped on the outside were large signs with warnings, *Do Not Enter!* Deep work requires quiet and privacy. A few candles were lit, giving just enough light for us to see each other.

I shared a simple guided practice that was meant to help us access a deeper life experience of heart centered touch than would ordinarily be available.

We sat in silence and darkness. The candles glowed. The background music—soft drumbeats—sounded like a distant heart. Not the beat of our mother's heart as we were nurtured, nor the beat of our father's mind as we were disciplined for battles of life, but the return of the beat to awaken our own heart and the healer within.

Each physician paired off with a partner, and then they sat in chairs, facing each other, creating together a row of six facing a row of six. Twelve physicians together, their hearts opening.

My voice softened, lowered and shifted to an inward call: "Awakening now, releasing your outer awareness from what you are seeing—the surface of things—release your thoughts and slowly close your eyes."

Awareness now releasing its connection to thoughts...

Breath now fully relaxing, releasing all tension from the body...

Centering now on the heart...

And connecting deeper and deeper into the heart; surrendering to its depth; feeling the warmth, seeing the light and sensing the calm.

"Breathing together, feeling the heart together, creating a space and place within together. Tuning in together, shifting together, heightening and augmenting our individual capacities to heal..."

The unifying energies, from our centering together, filled the room. My voice continued to guide, giving ample time for connection to the images, events or people the heart would reveal to them.

"Remember all the people our hands have touched over the years..." Pausing and waiting.

"All the babies who touched us as we touched them..."

"The births, the waters breaking free and spilling over our hands; their heads emerging, our hands serving as holy receptacles..."

"Remember, feel into the hands and the memories they carry." Pausing and waiting in the darkness.

"Now open your eyes slowly and with a soft gaze look at your hands with the tenderness of your heart, with its compassion."

"Feel their inherent beauty, their unending love and service."

"Placing awareness simultaneously on the heart center and the hand, remember the elders whose hands you held when death came, how they graced your hands with their last touches."

"Remember."

"Now allow your hands to be the conduit for the heart's unconditional love. Feel a sense of connection with your heart, as if a golden flowing light was coming from the heart and into your hand. Energy will follow the image. Allow your hands to be free to express this energy of unity and the love of the healer..."

The ancient mystery of blessing (touching with the heart) was brought to its full power through the intention and readiness of all of the participants. I had been holding a bottle of oil, lightly scented and warm, in anticipation of this moment.

"Now, open the left hand to receive," I said.

In the darkness, each waiting left hand received drops of warm, scented oil.

"Now allow your right hand to slowly move to the oil, and as if gifting the left hand, lightly and gently, spread the oil slowly over its entirety. Do this as if this was the last time you were to touch your body, the last time you were to show your love to it. As if your right hand were an extension of your heart, feel deeply into the tissue, sensing the gifting and awareness moving into the tissues, under the surface, touching every last cell, into the center of the hand, every cell being touched with awareness..."

I paused in the darkness as all the physicians came to completion, left hands resting in right hands. Then I moved behind one of the rows to drop more oil into the left hands of those six physicians.

Then I said, "Now take the right hand of your partner across from you and prepare to gift them with healing touch as deeply as you did your own."

"Watch your hand and remain connected to your heart. Fully gift the entire hand of your partner; connect to the sensations of your hand's energy moving into the other's hand. Use the lightest of touch to sense into their hands."

Then the other row of physicians who had been receivers became the givers.

"As you've gifted your own hand, so now give and gift the other's hand."

Each physician gave and received from the heart that day. Silence and darkness and the distant drum/heartbeat continued for another ten minutes, as eyes closed again to allow integration of what had occurred.

And then as the energy of the drumbeat reverberated throughout the room, my awareness was strangely pulled away from the group, as I deeply felt into a remembrance of Dave, my old friend the cardiac surgeon. So deeply, it almost felt as if he was in the room with me. I smiled as I remembered the gift of the heart's healing capacities he'd wanted to share with the medical profession and recognized how that gift and that sharing was now becoming reality.

The silence beyond the drumbeats continued. Images came to some, feelings to others. Tears began flowing quietly. We could heal and feel compassion on this level—it was an innate quality just waiting within us. In this place, colleagues and fellow travelers felt, validated and honored the unconditional love of the healer through touch. Then, gradually opening our eyes, we left inner reality to return to the outer world and its reality.

The music faded; the room lights returned slowly. We stretched our bodies; a few of us wiped away remaining tears. Some looked around the room as if wondering where they were, as if this was a strange new place.

After a break, we reconvened in a circle. On the floor, in the middle of our circle I placed a large crystal glass bowl of water that held a red rose on its surface.

A natural quietness came to the circle, and then comments on the experiences and images that had occurred began.

Mark, a hospice physician, spoke first about a vision he had: "I was in a great building, a temple of sorts for healing. It was one of the first gatherings of great physician teachers, when the first surgeries took place. There was a glass dome above, and I was near the center of the room, amongst them." His arms and eyes opened wide, expressing his yearning to share the experience, the gift, he'd received from his heart connection within.

His smile flashed unendingly; his body moved restlessly; both of his legs bounced up and down rhythmically; as if dancing in his chair.

Then Frank, the white-haired elder, tried to speak. He hesitated, gulped, took a deep breath and then sighed.

"You did it," he said to Mark, his right hand lifting as he pointed his quivering index finger across the room to Mark, who had been his partner for the healing experience. Frank averted his eyes, and then they began to fill with tears. "You did it," he said again, looking at Mark once more. Still pointing as if what had happened wasn't possible, as if no one but "the stranger" could have broken through the hardened armor of years of being a physician, as if this were an event to be feared and avoided or would result in dire consequences, or was simply not possible.

He said, "I've never been touched like that before." His pointing finger now bent and his hand now drooped slightly, as if too heavy to hold up. "He has the gift," Frank said, now beginning to choke, then clearing his throat over and over. His voice broke, weakening. "I have always given in my life. I... I never knew how to accept from another."

Frank searched for his breath. His left hand then came up from underneath to cup the right, supporting it, his right index finger bending more, no longer able to point to the "other," coming back to unite with the other three fingers. He pulled his hands back to himself, his right slowly opening to his own weathered face, all fingers uncurling naturally, all fingers touching his own right cheek. His eyes closed, tears flowing through and around his fingertips and over his own flesh. He breathed deeply, his head moving slightly from side to side.

His breath slowly returned, one long breath following another. His eyes opened as he returned to us, his hands gathering the healing moisture from his face, then coming down together, passing over his heart, over his body and coming to rest on his own thighs. Then, turning his head, he looked and smiled at everyone in the circle.

A moment later Ernie spoke: "I lost my daughter eight years ago, and I was deserted by even my closest friends and colleagues. No one was there for me."

He shed tears now, free of guilt, shame and anger. "You all understand," he said. And we waited silently, with open hearts, as his tears of pain transformed into tears of joy. Some of those present just looked at their hands, perplexed now, not saying much. Some seemed lost to the experience. Each had received to a unique degree.

Collectively, we visited a place where healers and champions of the heart gather and where the wisdom of the soulful elder is heard. Together we opened our hearts and experienced unexpected moments of unconditional love, a healing presence, innate harmony and compassion.

For a brief time, we had touched deeply and connected expansively through our common journey, yearnings, wounds and wholeness. We were becoming energy savvy, as we touched a vision beyond understanding, and in that moment, made it real. It was the realization that where we focus our awareness indeed, energetically, manifests our reality. This was a place to begin—a reflection of our inner-shared desires to heal and be healed.

The movement from heart centered presence to heart centered touch and then heart centered infusion had occurred. The use of hands as a vehicle to deepen healing was becoming more and more available. Infusing the heart's energy was the next gift of the emerging healer in us all.

It was another great gift from life; the emerging capacity to *infuse* the heart's energy *into* our own bodies and *infuse* it mutually with others whose hearts are open to giving and receiving.

There were parting embraces as the doors to the heart centering experience began to close.

Monday would be arriving soon, and everyone would be putting on their white armor again, as it must be, but it would be armor that was a little lighter. For we had all been renewed and rejuvenated by connecting to the "healing waters" called heart energy and been filled on the inside behind the armor. And there was now the capacity to shift anywhere and anytime to feel the warmth inside and hold a centered presence for self and others as called for—to become champions of the heart.

Over two years passed, teaching and integrating these energetic concepts in workshops with physicians, nurses and other allied health care professionals. I began to write about the stories that so moved me. I thought I knew the answer to our challenges, yet life was ready to bring me more personal lessons about the heart and the struggles associated with liberating its full power of unifying energy. Once again it came in the form of addictive behavior and its attendant yearning for change.

10
Suffering Made Visible

Our minds can't release the suffering they create.

"Dr. Gil, this phone call is for you, and he's very mad," the unit clerk said with a grimace.

"It's about Emma his daughter, who you saw yesterday."

I returned to my office, trying to prepare myself, to remain in charge and calm.

Seconds later, another physician's angry voice demanded, "What the hell is wrong with you? Are you trying to kill my daughter? How could you give her medication? Don't you guys ever check things out? Didn't you check her wrists to see the cuts? Didn't you know she just tried to commit suicide the night before? She's tried five times this year..."

"I didn't know," I replied, trying to hold steady amid the barrage of angry word-spears. I easily remembered her from the busy day before: a stunning young woman, everything about her was "just right," beautiful, long blonde hair, makeup perfectly applied, the latest faintly maroon lipstick. She'd been wearing a pink, long-sleeved blouse that hid the cuts and a short tight black skirt and had made two very common complaints: headaches and anxiety.

She'd pleaded, "You have to help me with my panic attacks," and then added, "I just haven't been able to sleep. Please help me. My migraines are intolerable." And then she wept.

"I've been dealing with this for years," she said, looking right at me, not averting her eyes. "I have an appointment with a new psychiatrist in two weeks, but my prescriptions ran out."

She was a college student, and unfortunately it was the weekend; it would be difficult to confirm her problems that day since her doctor was in another state.

The pill most commonly prescribed for this often-crippling condition of anxiety is Xanax. I trusted her; I'd treat her symptoms with a prescription of pain medication and a small amount of anti-anxiety medication.

She said she'd taken that combination before, and it would work. She said, "Thank you so much."

That night she tried to sleep again. She took all the pills with alcohol. She was seeking the eternal sleep. Her attempt however, was unsuccessful, and resulted in another ER visit at a nearby hospital—the same one she'd gone to the other time when she'd cut her wrists—and now another round of stomach pumping.

Now I replied to her father, "I am so sorry. I didn't sense it in her, and she wasn't on our list of drug seekers."

She was new to our emergency room. A few who are determined enough always slip through.

"You're all incompetent!" he ranted.

"You're going to make me bury my daughter," he yelled. My sense of guilt increased as his spear of judgment penetrated deeper. His anger bred more anger in him and in me, too.

Energies of anger heated up in my mind, and my mind placed steel tipped arrows, spears and swords into the fire, preparing to hurl sharp thoughts and words back into him.

I wanted to scream back and meet his anger, but blame and a fateful envelope from a lawyer would come next if that happened. It would say, in effect, "You're unworthy. You screwed up."

Don't lose it here, Gil, I thought. A few deep breaths came, a moment of calm, and my heart warmed again. "What can I do for you?" I asked aloud, shifting out of anger, as my heart opened to the crisis he was dealing with. Soon I felt centered and grounded again. The anger inside me subsided, and I lost my desire to hurl the energies of anger back at him. My mind's need to counter-attack in order to preserve "my integrity" gave way to the heart's presence.

He wasn't really angry with me; he was frustrated and caught in the futility of trying to save his daughter and keep her from doing it again. He'd shouldered the agonizing frustration and guilt of being unable to control her life and keep her from doing what she desperately wanted to do. Despite wealth, power, knowledge and his strong-willed attempts, he couldn't save this person who was so precious to him. Even as a father, he couldn't force things to be different.

The energies of anger continued—words, filled with anger hurled at me from hundreds of miles away. Then a pause came, a hesitation, and the last words, "Well, don't do it again."

The energies of anger hung in the air for some time, and then insight began to clear them away.

He knew no other way to react, I realized. He felt hopelessness and utter helplessness under that anger. Through his anger and lashing out, he was holding himself together, keeping himself from descending into a well of grief. It was his only way of being with what he couldn't really control.

He knows no other way to react, I reflected. *Ah, but neither do I, except for the moments when my heart holds me steady.*

Later, while I sat quietly contemplating this encounter, grateful for my heart's intervention, a spontaneous image came to me. It was as if I were in her room, observing her the night she was cutting herself. She was sitting alone, calmly holding the razor blade against her skin. She made a few light cuts; then, losing her fear, she placed the sharp corner of the blade on her wrist once again and pressed down harder. The blade sliced through the surface of the skin, filleting it open. She waited and watched for something to emerge from beneath the surface. Finally, blood flowed out. Shifting the razor to the other hand, she sliced the other wrist just as deliberately and calmly.

For a moment, the stillness and revelations while watching her blood stream down and drip off the sides of her hands must have alleviated some pain. She would have been calm in the moment, fulfilling some deep purpose and meaning by the act, some reassurance of the presence of feelings inside the body that the pain in the cut skin conveyed. Upon seeing the blood, some deeper momentary validation of life must have arisen, assuring her that what was done was enough. She was saved for the time being by the appearance of that blood. Indeed, I sensed, that the sight of her heart's tears for her was enough. She had no need to cut deeper—this time—no need to go in to the darkness any further.

Her yearning and suffering to live more deeply was so intense, and her despair of not finding it was so great. Was there nothing that could save her?

The ER can be a strange place. In one room, someone fights desperately to die, as if some wonderful thing might happen through death that can't be touched while the person's still alive. Someone commits suicide with a parting message that's joyful. Finally having made the decision and releasing the burdens of outer living, the person comes to complete peace with the fulfillment of their decision. In the next room, someone dying of a horrid illness fights desperately to live, as if something or some moment might still be touched in this life that will make it tolerable and leave them alive and whole...

Others continue to live miserable, depressed and anxious lives, covering their pain with a pleasant facial mask and with, "I'm doing fine," even though their hearts and souls ache so much in private that, in a way, these people were already dead. Their bodies like empty shells that move through an unchanging everyday landscape that is parched and deserted, with only a cactus here or there, without anything meaningful to touch.

And then there are the slow deaths—deaths by addiction, and not just alcohol or drug addiction, but addiction to something our promised land, the land of plenty and outer success, had never seen before (not even 30 years ago), but that was now extremely common: early death due to obesity.

Consider this woman in her early 50s, no more than 5'2" tall, weighing over 350 pounds. Barely able to walk, she was now becoming wheelchair-bound, or more likely, bound to a Rascal (a motorized four-wheel scooter), since she wouldn't be able to physically push herself in a wheelchair. She was taking 24 medications daily, including five herbal supplements, over one thousand pills a month; to treat her symptoms of diabetes, high blood pressure, elevated cholesterol, anxiety, depression, constipation, urinary incontinence, early kidney disease, early congestive heart failure, insomnia and allergies. Her enlarged legs appeared as if they were going to explode. The skin of her legs had become thick, blotched and leather-like in the body's attempts to hold against the pressure inside, but still it was splitting apart everywhere, weeping in many areas and showing early signs of infection.

Her lower abdominal wall hung down about a foot below her waist, reddened now with infection. I knew the scenario well. Amputations of her legs would probably begin soon, and movements from bed to chair would be done with a Hoyer lift, which is a mini-crane for humans that held a large, stiff, hammock-like device under the patient. Then, of course, she'd face prolonged hospitalizations and great risk for even more infection.

Upon seeing people like this, at first my judgment would arise, but I'd do my best to keep it secret and well hidden. *How can someone do this to their body?*

And then my anger would come. *Can't she see what she needs to do?*

But then I'd switch to the other self, the familiar self, Dr. Gil, the caring physician in the white coat and provide the expected response by finding a way to manage and attack the symptoms.

I smiled reassuringly. "It looks like your blood sugars need adjusting, and we'll have to keep you in the hospital for a while to fight the infection. But we'll get you back home soon."

Sadly, for this woman, it was too late for great change. We'd successfully micromanaged every one of her "problems" with great effort. Her blood sugars weren't too high or too low; she was balanced fairly well. Powerful medications regulated her cholesterol, which was now just right. Medication helped her sleep. Medication brought her up out of depression, and medication brought her down from her anxieties, so chemically she was as emotionally balanced as could be expected. Medication made her bowel movements just right, not too firm and not too loose. Medication kept her blood pressure from being too high, and we also regulated it to make sure it didn't go too low. Again, it was just right. Everything—every testable disorder and dis-ease that we could see—was being regulated and was just right. Using many specialists, each "attacking one of her problems," our dis-order and dis-ease management was perfect, and yet something was drastically amiss.

The main issue, the underlying core issue responsible for the vast array of symptoms, remained a mystery, and thus unaddressed.

My thoughts then moved to Gastric bypass surgery. Yet, I also knew in the next second that it couldn't be done in such a patient; it was too late. I knew we had nothing else to offer, and talking about her weight would be only too painful, it was completely off limits. No one could save her.

This was a slow, self-induced suicide, a self-destructive process due to excess of food, likely from the desperate hope that food filling the body, would satisfy a deeper hunger. She was trying so hard, but battle after battle had already been lost, and the war for her life was nearly over. She could not change.

Days later, I saw the opposite, also something rarely seen thirty years ago in America, the land of plenty. I stepped into a room to find someone alive, and yet dead. She had sparse, long, thinning blonde hair, sunken cheeks, sunken eyes, and her teeth were rotting from exposure to stomach acid from frequent vomiting. Her body was little more than skin covering bones. She weighed only 65 pounds. I checked first to make sure she was breathing. *Yes, there was still breath.* She was horribly emaciated. Her life force was leaving her, all caused by chronic self-induced vomiting.

Here was a slow suicide, a self-destructive process due to a lack of nutritious food. Seeking to fill a deeper hunger, she, too, was trying so hard. She hoped that through the loss of her flesh, she might ascend to some world where a greater love would fill the hunger. Her suffering in this world was now too great; she yearned and suffered for more. She was only 23 years old.

Her mother sat nearby, looking to me for any sign of hope. I could feel it. She was watching my every move, and yet I was drawn into her daughter's open eyes as she stared at the ceiling. Her eyes were empty, the product of a mind that had given up and a body that had no will to move. Gently my hand descended, touching the under surface of her wrist, concentrating now, in

my search to feel for the current of life. Nothing was felt. Shifting my fingers slightly, I concentrated even deeper. *Yes, there it was.* The pulse was still there, but thready, slipping away. Her heart was now in failure, dying. Her eyes also spoke of the shell she was—empty, with only the weak, distant beat of the heart in the dark emptiness
of her chest. No mother's love would be enough. No physician's skills would be enough to get her what she sought.

"We'll do our best," was all I could say, hoping, as I closed my eyes, that something inside her had suffered enough and would touch what she yearned for so much.

My hand lingered on her wrist, bringing me into compassion for the yearning and suffering of this young woman. I realized no one really understood what she was seeking. IVs would be started, we'd infuse her with fluids and try to keep her alive, and perhaps some tiny glimmer of hope might still yet appear, in the darkness, inside her dying body.

"We'll do our best," I said again.

And what of this man with severe obesity, hypertension and tension headaches? The half-empty liter bottle of Mountain Dew on the counter next to him prompted me to ask, "How much Mountain Dew are you drinking in a day?"

"Oh, about eight bottles," he replied nonchalantly.

"That's hard to believe," I replied while turning my head to his wife." She then nodded in the affirmative.

I think this is a record, I said to myself.

"Do you have any other sources of caffeine?" I said, still stunned by his reply.

"Well, I do have two pots of coffee before I start my day," he replied without hesitation, totally unaware of what he was doing to himself.

This is right up there with the man with chronic bronchitis that was smoking six packs of cigarettes a day, I thought to myself.

And in the land of plenty, filled with striving for more outer success, and all of the "super-sizing" it brought, the stories continued. Drug dealers supplied the expensive drugs needed to allay the unending emotional, psychological and mental pain of the many wishing to escape their known realities and inner emptiness or, at the very least, to make reality tolerable. The yearning and suffering in some became so intense that overdoses of that which helped to alleviate the pain and silent suffering became that which killed. What had been a friend betrayed and/or befriended too much, bringing death.

Families were torn apart by guilt, blame, anger and hopelessness.

Sometimes, when I felt the despair too deeply, it became too much. Hidden parts of me that felt the inconsolable pain and suffering that seemed as if it would last forever then said, *Let him die.* Sometimes it seemed my help only made things worse, prolonging the emotional pain of another by keeping him or her around. But wasn't it my duty to stop any attempts to die, to battle death, even put the patient in shackles if necessary?

Maybe it needed to be that way. I couldn't save them from what wanted to happen, from the endless yearning and despair. I couldn't save them from their self-critical, self-destructive mental programs that ran day and night. My role was to stabilize them when they came to the ER.

Everyone around this suicide mystery was desperately uncomfortable. Perhaps it was not completely the suicidal people they worried about, but also the personal fear that their own struggles with life would erupt dangerously simply from being so close to people who wanted to die.

I now came into a deeper appreciation for the stable role I held and how it protected me. From behind the white coat, I was able to offer those battling with symptoms of addiction and suicide a kind word, a touch of compassion, or some drug that would hold things together. To cure (control, remove or cut out) the outer symptoms and return people back to "normal" for a while was usually possible to some degree. However, the deepest issues of the crisis remained untouched. The deeper wounds seemed unapproachable and best left alone—as if they were too powerful, too difficult to understand, or too painful to open to with the ordinary means available.

A deeper understanding of death was about to reveal itself however, as I too began to experience a difficult struggle between my mind and the forces holding me in its reality and the reality of my heart that was also calling to me. It was the darkest of times for me, a struggle with the darkness of the unknown, beyond my known outer life.

11

Darkness

Our encounters with the darkness of the unknown within,
come into our lives for a reason.

My most intense encounter with darkness started
unexpectedly during a storm. Wet snow was falling on that late
March night, covering the promise of spring I'd felt earlier in the
day. The wind whipped around big, fat flakes. The storm had left
the road home empty and desolate, and at times my headlights
could barely penetrate the swirling white. I strained to see the
path through the storm, which was now slippery and treacherous.
I was returning home from my first day at a distant hospital. It
was so far from where "Dr. Gil" had practiced for over 20 years
prior that I somehow felt like a mercenary, fighting medical
battles in some foreign land.

In the midst of that storm and darkness, however, I suddenly
felt as if I had lost my way. Lost my connection to that yellow
brick road to the interior place that I felt was calling me.

The storm became so strong it forced me to pull onto a side
road and wait for its intensity to pass. There the wipers continued
to fight the snow, as it also began to melt and turn into streams
of moisture going down the windshield. I struggled to hold back
the unexpected thawing of my frozen inner feelings. When the
private tears of sorrow finally ended, a deep and lonely
contemplation of life ensued.

It was as if my life, though successful by every measure on
the outer level, was ironically a failure as something was still
missing or unknown.

It was not depression (low energy), but what has been called
the dark night of the soul. It was a time of despair; a feeling that
the essence of life would never be found.

Reviewing my life, I could see only the things that could be
labeled "failure." And so despair also revealed itself as a sense of
permanent loss of essence, a loss so profound that at moments it
was overwhelming. Despair was now my constant companion.

It all, however, remained hidden inside the white coat, which I still depended on. Others saw only the man in control, with his white armor, with the answers, having a good day...

Even in my journals, which I tended to daily, I avoided writing down these feelings and skirted around any new expressions of my struggle to understand the relationship between darkness and death and living anew. Death? What kind of death? Death of a reality? Was there a difference? If so, the difference could not yet be separated.

Keep the struggle a secret, a voice inside kept saying. *Don't talk about it to anyone. No one can do anything about it, anyway. No one wants to hear about it. Act as if it doesn't exist.*

But the darkness of the unknown remained, as if demanding exploration once again.

Over and over again, life was about facing our demons and our darkness over and over again?

One day the darkest moment of my life came. I was alone and thousands of miles from home. The sense of loss of meaning and direction in life was overwhelming. I was driving a rental car through a dark rainy night in Phoenix after at tending a conference that ironically was about "healing."

The roads were slippery, and all I could think of was a recurring image of heading to the highway. An image that had come to me many, many times in the weeks prior, as if rehearsing it over and over, to end it all, to find a semi to drive into, or if not then a concrete pillar. Death it seemed was the only way to find peace in this type of darkness.

Calm came as I sensed the peace that would come with death. *Everyone will be able to go on with their lives,* my mind rationalized. The calm continued as I drove past the neon signs blurred by the rain trickling down my side window. Lights announced the excitement of food, beer, women and gambling. The window continued its silent weeping. The last stoplight before the highway came, pausing, as lights went from red to green, over and over and over. A few cars now and then drove around mine. Stuck at the stoplight, my past life flashing in front of me, taking me up to the moment of impending completion. It was fine; it would be OK.

Then, unexpectedly, my self-absorption gave way to reviewing the names of all those dear to me. *Yes, everyone will go on. It will be all right.*

Peace would come through death. It was a strange calm I felt with the finality of my decision.

But then I uttered my daughter's name again, and I choked, and coughed and couldn't catch my breath. Suddenly I was overwhelmed with tears of sorrow. It was as if my body was convulsing with grief. *She will not recover. The path of pain and suffering will continue unbroken.* I felt her presence and said her name over and over.

Then while repeating her name, suddenly, it was as if a single ray of light was shot through my armor and into the center of my chest. My chest ached and heaved again, but now tears of sorrow ironically were being transformed into tears of gratitude—there was a reason to live!

With time I moved, the car was no longer stuck, it went into the parking lot instead of to the highway. My chest was filled with light and love. Gratitude, gratitude, gratitude for life and for the embodied lesson that had flowed through me.

Life had prepared me for months and then taken me into the darkness (the unknown/unconscious realms behind our ordinary awareness). There it showed me that the answer to the darkness was really the light called love and our capacity to connect with others through it. It would take many more years for me to integrate that experience (and more clearly understand *the death/release of our old two-dimensional reality and an old self* that we in some way, are all seeking to release, in times of intense darkness).

The darkness left. My heart centering practice had been lost, but was found again in a new and expanded way. With it came an additional petition to understand the darkness or unknown aspects and struggles of our lives in a more expanded way. Life shifted, and it became important for me to engage darkness, not push it away or label it as wrong or bad. I began exploring the darkness as best I could, its deeper meaning now opening to me. The light inside darkness (enlightenment) was now shining more and more.

It was back to writing, art, movement and listening to my dreams. Slowly an emerging "energetic" understanding of our life as an unfolding journey and the phase called "engaging the darkness," began to reveal itself.

Ironically, the encounter with darkness also began to transform my capacity to be with others in similar situations. More and more, others began to trust me, confide in me, as I held a silent heart centered presence for them. I could say, "I know" and hold a place of compassion for them. The heart centering practice had expanded to give me the resources to hold a place of calm in the midst of the more powerful storms others were experiencing. I could hold onto the light, trusting and waiting until the other felt or saw the light also, in the midst of their darkness. I would see again and again, heart centering and the sharing of the heart's power through silent presence, gave deep meaning to the struggles and darkness in every life.

Opening the heart again, renewing my connection to it again, was opening me to both the depths of sorrow and joy. When the meaning of the struggle in others and myself was revealed, the joy was often profound. Barriers of separation from our hearts were breaking down as never before.

It had been a long time since Rose, but I still frequently thought about what had happened to her in the darkness of death that she had faced, and the healing and radiance that emerged from it. *What had made that evening in the ER so unique, so empowering, so healing, so joy filled? What was it between her daughter and myself that I'd felt the night we embraced two months later?*

I must write about this.

Writing now became a new passion in my life; the core of the writing involved our personal and collective journey of healing through crisis and into wholeness. There had to be a scientific answer to the experiences and energies of healing/unification and a way to prove it, write about it, embody it more fully, and bring it to the world in a way that could benefit us all, here and now. Four years passed in intense mental research and writing. My intellect once again began to take over, as if demanding an intellectual answer.

As my relationship with writing deepened and required more and more of my time, I sometimes wondered about the intensity of my searching and writing. Had I, like so many of the people I had seen in the ER, simply created an intensity to searching as a substitute for an addiction. My insomnia was worsened, caused by working unusual hours, and now, with the added intensity of writing, my body became fatigued and burned out.

Lost again?

This continued until the face of addiction and suffering and yearning revealed itself more clearly, as metal crashed into metal once again.

12
My Turn

We all get many turns to find our heart.

My turn came almost exactly nine years after Dave's death, when, fatigued after a long shift, I was driving through the darkness of late night and fell asleep...

April 16, 2002:

Metal crashing against metal, forces pushing the dashboard inward... A sudden awakening, all breath gone, chest feeling compressed... Jolted into another world, the gray haze, the quiet of the in-between world in the passageway to death, as if no longer in a body, separated...

The van rolling away and down toward a steep curb... Still no breath, and then another jolt... Pain shooting through the front of my chest, taking me out of that inner world... and then, strangely, struggling for the first breath, my chest constricted and empty, totally empty, unable to breath, as if paralyzed in the state of emptiness...

You have to breathe. Breathe! Feeling the body and chest unable to break the paralysis... Nothing happening... *Breathe! Breathe!*

Suddenly, I wondered, *Is this the same time in April when Dave died?* And then it was time—time to break free and open to breath...

The first gasp felt like a hot, sharp knife, *aaahhh, aaahhh...* that cut in to the center of my chest... I breathed in, and then held it, not wanting to feel the pain of movement again... Holding the breath, both my hands reached for the center of my chest... *Oh, my God. Oh, my God, oh!* And only then came the realization that I'd just been in an accident...

My memory of the day returned clearly. It had been a beautiful sunny spring day in early April. I'd had a long day at work and had made a midnight departure. I'd refused to drink caffeine so that sleep could come more easily when I got home about an hour and a half later. I remembered the grogginess, the van accelerating, and then…

The carbon dioxide and dust from the air bags was clearing. My glasses, along with everything else, were scattered above and below the dash of my smashed window. I pushed my way out against the jammed door, slowly and painfully making my way to the center of the intersection where the driver of the other vehicle was moaning and holding his chest as I was holding mine. He was short, black-haired and in his 30s. As if lightheaded, he rolled sideways out of his car door, right down on to the road and on his back. He grimaced and moaned without speaking, his hands also over the center of his chest. Still in my hospital scrubs, I bent down to touch him, to somehow help him with his pain as best as I could.

"You're going to be all right. Breathe slower if you can," I said, putting my jacket under his head. An ambulance was coming; I heard the sirens. "Hang in there. You're going to make it."

You have *to make it! Please make it. Please!*

There, in the middle of the night, in center of the crossroads, the paramedics pulled in, lights flashing everywhere.

As they quickly loaded him up, I said, "I'm sure he has broken ribs. Please check his breath sounds and make sure his lungs are okay, that he doesn't have a pneumo…" [a collapsed lung technically known as a pneumothorax].

When they turned to me, I said, "No, I don't want to go to the ER. I can take care of myself."

The pain now returned with a vengeance, but I wouldn't let it overcome me.

A police officer was kind enough to transport me to a motel about a mile away.

I called Janis. My sentences were short, like my breath. Talking was painful. Any breath was painful. But I said, "I'm just fine. Just a little banged up. No, don't come to get me. I'll be fine."

The motel bed was so hard, and my body so sore. I silently talked my way through the night.

Okay, breathe slow, slower. Careful, don't let it take over; don't let the pain overwhelm you. Stay in control. Concentrate and remain in control.

My lungs must be okay. I can still breathe. My heart, my heart—was it injured? I won't know without going into the ER. My pulse is okay now. It must be okay... I lay alone, worrying about my heart. Maybe it was bruised, just bruised...

With my eyes closed I tried to feel my physical heart, to sense the muscle on its surface, to see the bruising just under the painful rib above it.

And I wondered about the other man—would he be all right? Would he make it?... I sent out a prayer through the darkness of the night to the ER I knew he'd be going to, into the ER and its rooms of beds covered with white sheets, hoping it would find him and support him...

There was no sleep that night.

In the morning Janis arrived, and we went to survey my van. Its front was gone, leaving only a radiator squashed flat against the engine, the hood bent in half and buckled up over two feet, the window gone. Gnarled metal—a testament of how quickly life can change or be wiped out. I thought of Dave again, and the ironic intertwining of our lives...

Later that day I called the ER the other driver had been taken to. He'd be OK, they said, just broken and bruised ribs. A prayer in the middle of darkness had been answered, no one had to die.

But life continued its lessons for me.

Sleepless nights continued at home. Movement in the center of my sternum and a left rib next to it (right over the physical heart) confirmed I had fractures in those areas.

For ten days I got little rest and suffered from constant pain in my chest.

I told myself to keep concentrating, to be in control and not let the pain win.

With pain and sleep deprivation, my ordinarily rational thinking mind at times shifted to deep introspection...

I realized my yearning to find the answer through writing had become too intense. I had been constantly writing, as if writing was the answer, as if I would find "it." Then, I started thinking about finding "the answer" all the time. I was becoming more fatigued. Too much thinking and mentally trying to find "the answer" had nearly killed me!

So much time had passed, so little progress it seemed. In my own way I was hungry, like all the others I saw in the ER. Some dealt with the hunger with more food, power, wealth, possessions, external beauty, youth preservation, exercise, drugs (licit and illicit), substance abuse, gambling or sex. Some were addicted to reading, television, the internet, travel, winning, success, achieving goals, sports, spending, busyness, spirituality or religion. The list kept growing. Some were attached to trying to change others, blaming others, worrying, working, or the drama often involved family matters and power struggles. Some were even having children to fulfill some unmet need and then, a few years later, finding out it didn't. The latest was furiously intense video games that always had the same results—winning or losing. Games that left individuals exhausted, addicted to intensity itself, hands frozen to the controls. The list went on and on. Addictions, attachments and the underlying hunger were everywhere—in so many subtle and overt expressions. Yet no one, it seemed, could find "it" or really had the answer and was able to end the intense cycle of addictive behaviors.

I thought of all the patients I had once helped stop smoking, only to see some of them years later, weighing over a hundred pounds more than before. The addiction itself was not the root of the problem; it was the greater enigma—the yearning to satisfy an insatiable hunger—the emptiness that was trying to be filled. That was the true dilemma.

Here we were again, like so many years ago, despite all of the keys, steps, secrets, 3, 5, 7 and 12 step programs for change. These mentally directed and controlled switches, surface makeovers and outer changes did help stabilize our outer lives temporarily, but did not address the deeper hunger and emptiness, nor did it create a deeper understanding of their origins. We continued to remain attached to the belief that our minds could really change us and that the answer was "out there."

Many were going deep into debt from their addictions because the addictions were so powerful, the needs so great, the hunger so endless and mysterious.

What is my debt in time and energy? I thought. *What's the cost of addressing my hunger and yearning for a different life?*

No one is escaping. Yes, we were really all in this together. The intensity of our addictive patterning and behavior; the yearning, searching and personal inner sense of lack involved everyone to some degree. No matter how busy we kept ourselves or denied its existence, it's always there.

Then a new thought came, one I'd never contemplated before: *What if our addictions and attachments were serving us, something like friends, until something else unknown came along?*

What if our addictive lives aren't even problems, but signs, natural signs of an impending birth or emergence of something to come? What if our addictive relationships with substances or mental beliefs are always revealing the intensity of our hunger for something else? It seems that no matter what our outer persona is, we need an intimate friend, an addictive friend to carry on with us, a friend and a love even greater than that for another human, even a life-partner that filled our outer needs. Perhaps, even, no human could fulfill our growing intimate and inner needs as our addictions could.

Might our addictions walk with us to the edge, where we sense our outer bankruptcy and inner yearning and the increasing weight of the armor of beliefs we've carried, weighing us down, like a personal cross of sorts, pushing us down, until we have to turn elsewhere, until we awaken by turning inward for answers.

What if only this inward movement will release our mental relationships and attachment with our addictive friends and intensities of life. What kind of divorce would that be? What if the unburdened life was strangely different? What if we didn't need to use all our energy to support an addiction or the outer surface persona of our old self as it had been? Would it be like flying? Would our freedom to live and love as a new self, be that great?

Focusing so frequently on the pain in my chest ironically took me deeper and deeper into the understanding of addictions and addictive behavior. *Perhaps, in some strange way we just aren't able to understand, we aren't ready yet to let go of what was, our attachments, our beliefs, our sense of self, our old behaviors, or our addictions. They still all helped us cope and brought us a sense of stability in some strange way in this period of transition. What was still missing?*

But in the moment I knew what I had to do, I needed a break and I thought I could still control my "intense needs" to know.

Despite my chest pains, I walked to the writing room, grabbed the manuscript I'd worked on for over four years and threw it into the back of the upstairs closet, where it would collect dust over the coming years. In the moment, the final answer, I was sure, wouldn't come through my intellect and the written word; it was beyond that kind of understanding, and continuing to intensely write and search for the answer mentally would either burn me out or turn me into a road statistic some night.

After ten days, the pain and sleep deprivation became too much. I gave up and went to the same clinic where I'd once started as Dr. Gil to see Earl, my personal physician and friend, to help me with my symptoms. I was feeling like a banged-up failure.

"Earl, I need help," I said, releasing tears as I let myself break down for a brief moment. "I just can't take the pain anymore, and the loss of sleep has been unreal. I can't go on like this."

I was grateful for the pain medication and the ten sleeping pills he prescribed.

The ache continued for another two months. Life wanted to wake me up, to get my attention, to show me what I needed to focus on, and it was using a close encounter with death and an intimate reminder called *pain.*

Gradually my recovery began. My life again shifted away from trying to understand and look for outer answers.

Instead, I focused on breathing and understanding the deeper, yet very fundamental, message of the pain in the center of my chest.

I had been lost in the intensities of everyday life for some time, foolishly thinking that my search had led me beyond the patterns of attachments, addiction and yearning I had witnessed daily, but through the accident, I had found my heart again. Each morning I would again surrender, for a brief time releasing my attachment to my mind, returning to my practice of nourishing and being nourished by my heart center. As thousands of times before, every morning alone, while it was still dark, yet near the break of dawn, I went down the stairs to a room that became the heart of our house. Removing my shoes, I opened the door, walked slowly to the middle of the room and knelt on a small bench and connected again to my center.

One night a dream comes to affirm the inner journey:

It's dark and I am leaving my house that is an old farmhouse with bare wood, all paint now gone. The house is dark now as I step out with my jacket on and into a stiff wind. I am walking into the darkness, not knowing where I am going. It's fall, the trees are all bare and the wind is howling and filled with flying leaves. Soon, in the distance, I see a faint light. I continue to push forward with difficulty, as the wind and cold intensifies. I finally reach a large three-story building that is very modern, it is transparent as if made from thick glass, somewhat like a large hospital that is filled with over a hundred patient rooms.

The main door, to my surprise, is unlocked and I open it and begin to walk down a long corridor, passing many empty rooms, in fact the entire building was empty, so it seemed. I was walking toward the one room in the center of the building that had the light's glow coming through its slightly opaque walls. The door, on the left side of the corridor was at the far end of the room and was open. As I turned through the door and to the left I saw about forty men and women surrounding an elevated examination bed. There was a glowing light filling the room from the bed and illuminating them also. I sensed there was an adult on the bed, but could not see who it was. The circle began to open for me as the person closest to my left turned and said, "We've been waiting for you." The dream ends.

Our past, our current struggles, our future? The images affirmed the inner journey to the heart's center was indeed alive and well. It was a deeply personal message for me, as dreams always are. This one I felt was also for "us," a collective dream of our difficult journey of leaving the old ways of engaging life and embracing our new capacities to heal.

Outer events and encounters also began to shift likewise.

Ironically, one morning, later that summer, I saw a picture of Shauna Lee in the local newspaper. She was kneeling behind the prize lamb at the county fair, and her sister was standing and holding the lamb's head up with a harness. Shauna Lee had become a magnificent young woman. Her beautiful blonde hair was pulled back tightly, and her eyes sparkled with life. Yes, she was alive.

Her picture was a reminder to me of the importance of the inner journey, and the enrichment and empowerment that come from connecting with the center of the heart. Her visit to the ER had begun my connection and my journey into the heart. Within her image was a life of hope realized, joy manifested, and the impossible embodied.

Thank you, life, for Shauna Lee.

It was time to go deeper again.

Time to learn more...

Just as I had previously sought out the depressed to work with, I now sought out the opportunity and challenges to be with those in obvious addictive crisis, in great despair, or involved with the mystery of suicide. They were my great teachers now. The nursing staff assisted, often telling me, "This patient is for you."

On the road of healing, another patient came to teach...

13
Now I Know

*Coming home to our inner garden,
we find it in full bloom.*

The family car stopped at the emergency entrance; once again Diane was on the edge, wanting to live and yet with the same intensity wanting to die. She'd struggled all her life with drugs, alcohol and depression.

The nurse and someone from security rushed out to aid her.

The retching started as she shifted out of the passenger seat and into a wheelchair, and a pink emesis basin was quickly placed on her lap. As she entered the ER, her head and long black hair dropped backwards over the top of the wheelchair. Mouth gaping open, eyes rolling backward, her body went limp, slouching, and ready to slide off. The nurse rushed her through the department and headed to one of the larger rooms.

Her breathing was shallow; the protocol was that significant respiratory distress requires intubation.

Her mother quickly told me the tragic story as we stood near the entrance of the ER. Diane was intoxicated again and had taken two huge hits of cocaine that morning.

Three nurses went in to the room with her to get vitals, draw blood for chemical analysis, drug and alcohol levels and to prepare for intubation if she stopped breathing. I stepped in shortly thereafter and simultaneously felt the warmth in the center of my chest.

She retched and retched, stomach muscles tightening over and over. Spitting out the bitter green bile gave her momentary relief. Her eyes rolled off to the left, her head fell left, and then, jerking, her body fell to the left also.

I approached the examination bed. Exhausted, with pasty sweaty skin and strings of vomit on her hair and clothes, she somehow still managed to turn to the right, toward me, her right hand grasping the railing.

Our eyes locked for a moment. Her drowsiness and confusion suddenly shifted as I had something to say.

"You are a very spiritual person. You know there is a far greater way of loving and being in life, but you have no place to nourish that, no place to keep that alive, no one to support it. That's why you keep trying to kill yourself."

She said nothing, remaining still and focused. Then a brief episode of retching started, but she was more alert now, more awake. When she stopped I came closer and gently rested my right hand on her left shoulder and felt into our encounter and wondered why we were brought together.

"Can you take a few deep breaths for me?" I asked. She bent forward as my stethoscope slipped down to the back of her chest. I listened deeply and synchronized my breath with hers, and then focused, heard and felt the deeper rhythm of her heart; everything was going to be OK.

Her vitals and her breathing stabilized. Intubation wouldn't be needed, so I stepped out, leaving her in the care of the nurses in the room.

About ten minutes later, a thin lady in her late 70s with large, bluish-gray curls appeared. She stood in front of the nursing station, immaculately dressed in a white blouse and gray wool skirt and jacket. It was Diane's mother, who had been sitting in the corner of the trauma room at the time I stepped in.

"I'd like to see the doctor," she told the unit clerk. Overhearing the request, I stepped out to see her in the center of the hall. Turning toward me, she stood, one hand enfolding the other, her eyes inviting me closer.

She reached out to me with her weathered and frail left hand, palm up, and my right hand came down to rest on it. Then her right hand came down, gently covering mine. She pulled my hand closer to her, toward her heart.

Slowly, her right hand caressed the surface of mine—her bones and veins so easily seen through her paper-thin skin. Watching silently, our heads bowed, her tears flowed freely, falling downward as her hand gently moved back and forth over mine.

"I want to thank you for being so kind," she said. Then she paused for a few more tears.

She sighed, and her breathing calmed. "My daughter wants me to thank you. She's been in and out of institutions for over twenty years, battling alcohol and drugs. She's tried to commit suicide many times. She's had over fifteen doctors during those years. She wants me to tell you that you are the first doctor who ever understood." Silence followed, as a wise woman filled with a mother's love and a man still searching for answers embraced in the hallway of the ER.

Diane remained stable and was admitted to intensive care for close observation and treatment, leaving me again to ponder the mystery of our lives, our self-destructive behaviors and the simultaneous underlying yearning to die and live anew that was becoming more and more obvious to me as a dynamic that existed inside all of us to different degrees at different times—as if it was a destiny of sorts. Then I said to myself, *This experience with Diane will sustain me for months.*

I'd been reminded once again of the power of the heart's healing energies and wisdom. The embrace with Diane's mother reminded me of Rose's daughter and what we'd experienced between us.

Weeks passed, and then one morning when I came into the ER, a nurse said, "Someone's left something for you in your office."

A white porcelain vase stood at the center of my cubicle's desk, overflowing with wild asters: deep purple petals with yellow centers. To the left of the flowers was a white porcelain cherub, its wings touching the ground, sitting on its bent left leg, right knee up, arms outstretched, looking upward toward the flowers.

In an envelope in front of the vase was a card with the image of a golden vase filled with purple asters, containing a note:

Dear Dr. Burgstede,

Thank you. You saved my life. Now I understand. I don't need to kill myself any more... My life has been blessed. I know everything is going to be all right.

Diane

I recalled the words we'd shared that day: "You are a very spiritual person. You know there is a far greater way of loving and being in life, but you have no place to nourish that, no place to keep that alive, no one to support it. That's why you keep trying to kill yourself."

As fate would have it, about six months later, I stepped into an exam room to see a patient for coughing, only to find a woman grinning widely. I was taken aback somewhat by her cheerful presence until she asked, "Don't you remember me?" She continued to smile. "I'm Diane, the one who came in with the overdose last fall."

"Yes, yes, I remember you," I said, amazed. Recalling the scene in my mind, I returned her smile.

She described how her life had changed. The drugs she'd once so desperately needed, she needed no longer. A deep sense of meaning and passion for her new life of service to others had replaced them. Other than a viral infection with some wheezing, her body was vibrant and healthy.

I remembered the vase, the flowers, the cherub and the note that said, "Now I understand."

And at that moment I again remembered the depth of the hunger for a greater love and realized that no hunger can be satisfied until the hunger for the heart is satisfied. I remembered the need for others to share love with, and I remembered the love that was infused through her mother's hands into mine and the power of our embrace. I remembered that there was a garden inside each of us...

And yet, the ER continued to fill up more and more with erupting symptoms of anxieties, depressions, addictions and associated dis-eases and dis-orders. The battle to cure these symptoms was intensifying with more prescriptions, more counseling and more surgeries. Those paralyzed with deep depression needed relief to become functional again. Those possessed with intense addictions and obsessive thought patterns needed relief. Those blinded by old beliefs of low self-worth, who were now filled with anxiety, were unable to do anything due to fear and needed relief. They all needed relief from their symptoms.

But a new light was revealing itself more frequently in the moments I spent with them. Indeed, more moments and more encounters took place with those whose protective armoring (that held in other emotional energy), was becoming more transparent. The armor offered less resistance to the unifying energy from the center!

Each encounter, each taste of this new energy, each image of personal wholeness reminded me, if only for a moment, that something very profound was beginning to happen inside all of us—more and more individuals were feeling the heart's power.

A year would pass, during which I would again fill myself regularly with doses of heart energy in a morning practice of centering, and then another empowering lesson would arrive in the form of an encounter with yet another beautiful human being.

14

Dorothy's Joy

To embrace one's own life fully is to then fully
awaken to see the beauty in everything.

Vibrant and outgoing, Dorothy was often seen about town wearing a red coat and dark red shoes.

Dorothy was ninety-two years old when she taught me about the beauty of life. Dorothy was once a second grade teacher, a job she loved dearly, she thought that a good education was the most important gift we could give our children. Dorothy had her share of tragedy—the loss of an eighteen-year-old daughter in a car accident, the loss of her husband to cancer, living alone for ten years, with remaining family members far away. And yet she had a remarkable enthusiasm in her continued service to life, working for human rights and women's rights for equality around the world.

"Empowered women and empowered men, walking together, that's what will change this world," she often said, as she lamented the current state of conflicts in the world, due to endless power struggles between men and the unending need for wars.

"They desperately need our help," she also frequently said, and then followed it with, "we must get on with it by educating men and women in a different way."

That was her main dream and hope, of someday seeing empowered women and men working together for the children of the world, for a different and better future for all.

Seemingly alone, and yet fulfilled in so many ways, she was always expressing thanks for life and seeing the beauty of life. Even the death of her husband was seen as a gift, for though dearly missed, "being alone allowed me to find out who I was outside of the role of being a wife."

Her health was remarkable, and so one day I was moved to ask her, "Why are you so enthused about life and in such great health?"

"Well," she said, "Every morning, since my daughter died, I begin my day like this."

Her hands slowly came up and into a self-embrace. Her eyes closed and her head bowed slowly, her body softening more and more with each breath. Shoulders softening and dropping, jaw softening, face softening. Then slowly, deeply and softly her voice began, "I love you, I love you so very much, I love you, I love you so very, very much." Head moving slightly from side to side, "I love you, I love you so very, very much."

Voice of her heart continuing to reveal its love, becoming deeper and softer, deeper and softer, then becoming only the movement of lips, then going completely inwardly, no visible outer sign left of the healing words the heart had called out.

I watched in silence as my heart center, too, was now fully in my awareness, as if my heart, too, had called me inward into an energetic communion. I, too, was breathing with her, my head, too, was slightly bowed.

Stillness came to her whole body. Silence and stillness. Deeper and deeper into the center her awareness went. And then it came as a subtle wisp of wind might touch our cheek and awaken us, as love spread across her face, alighting it, and she sighed gently, as if deeply lost in the fragrance of a rose. Lost and then found in the garden of the eternal now. Lost in a silent and still communion with her heart that lasted over three minutes.

Then a slight rocking of her body began. Her hands then ever so slowly, gently and lovingly moving up and down over her shoulders, blessing her own body. Her head moving slightly from side to side, in ever deepening gratitude for the self-nourishing touch of the heart. And then after a few eternal moments, her head turned and her cheek rested over her right hand. Cheek and hand caressing each other. Moving slowly and tenderly. I had watched patiently, heart-fully.

Then slowly her head came up, her eyes opened and she looked from deep inside and straight into me, as she threw her arms open to her sides. Smiling radiantly and saying, "Do you think that might be it?" and then she laughed, as her eyes squinted and her head moved from side to side. I grinned and nodded my own head up and down in agreement.

Even into her mid-nineties before the diagnosis of her cancer, when I would visit her, she would still be pointing out a flower, or a tree, or reciting a poem, or speaking of the sacredness of the human body, and remarking, "Isn't it beautiful? Doesn't it just make you want to weep?" And sometimes she would.

When asked about her healthy eating habits, she replied, "The body is a temple, why would you want to treat it any other way."

She died at ninety-seven, electing to have no surgery or other therapy for her leg cancer but to die at home, doing "my work as long as I can." Near the end, I spent an evening caring for her. She only weighed seventy pounds; she was so weak she could only talk with great difficulty, struggling to share, trying to put a few raspy words together.

She delivered three messages to me during that night. Words I could only hear by holding my left ear just inches above her mouth, patiently waiting as her heart insisted the messages be delivered, even as the voice and body struggled to make it possible.

The first of the three messages came at two o'clock in the morning. Each single word required rest thereafter. One word at a time, and with time coming together as one sentence, "I want to give you the courage to trust people," which in the moment, I realized, was to trust the deeper resources and capacities we all carry to love and live life more fully. She was speaking again of the light that exists behind everyone's armor of beliefs and actions, no matter how they might be judged or carry themselves on the outside.

Exhausted by the effort, she slept for another hour and then was able to share again. It was one of her favorite sayings that reflected her joy of living, "I'm happy as a lark," and she smiled as best she could, for one so close to death. Her eyes closed after the delivery of the second message.

As I prepared to leave in the morning before another caretaker came, her thin arms came up to pull me toward her...

The past and the future released.
Heart gently resting next to heart. Heart to heart.
Centers ignited and igniting.
And the garden of life was full and radiant again.

She whispered into my ear again. They were her last words. The two most beautiful words in the English language, "Thank you."

Dorothy died peacefully at home in her bed shortly thereafter.

Many months later I visited her grave. The small flat gravestone was a testament to her life, it had these words written on it, "My cup runneth over."

Thank you, Dorothy, for teaching us through your life, to no longer see only the surface of things and people, but to be opened so deeply that hidden beauty is revealed and liberated in an experience of wholeness that can only be called a radiance of love.

Dorothy had awakened to the deeper beauty of life from time to time. She had gone beyond the struggle between the old ways of just engaging life mentally and the new ways of trying to live from her heart. She had found the way to experience the wholeness of life over and over. Her "Well of Life Transforming Water" was filled with life rejuvenating energy that was deep, clear and filled with joy, and was shared in our every encounter.

Dorothy had found her way home, and gone beyond the fear of love to experience its radiant liberation.

Now in her remembrance, she is still telling us to trust our hearts: to hear the call to come home now, to become empowered with others, to find renewed purpose and passion in life, to come into gratitude and into joyful service to life, even to the last breaths, even as many others were still suffering and could not see, hear or embrace it...

15
Fierce Guardians

Fierce guardians remind us to
take care of our own stuff first.

Suffering that can't be touched.

The chart said this about Ms. Smith: "Painful knee for eight months, worse during the past week, especially when walking."

I stepped in to the room to find a woman with her head bent and her left hand pressed against her forehead, crying with heavy sighs and stuttering breath. Her left hand moved down to meet her right hand, and she began rubbing both sides of her right knee.

She moaned, "The pain is getting worse. I've tried to stay off it, and that hasn't helped. The pain medications don't help. You have to help me, no one else has!"

Her history revealed a slow progression of pain over the past months that had worsened with exertion. I examined the knee and found no sign of infection or clot in the leg, and recent X-rays showed some arthritic changes but had been unremarkable in pointing to any stress fracture or other abnormality.

I said, "Your pain is most likely from degenerative arthritic changes. We can give you more pain medication..."

"I don't want more pain medication," she replied, her face anguished. "I want it *fixed*."

Short of a referral to an orthopedist to discuss knee replacement, there wasn't much else I could do. She was 43. Most orthopedists would be hesitant because the replacement would wear out sooner, and knees can't keep being replaced indefinitely.

But I thought I knew the underlying problem and source of the pain, and I thought I knew what would be best for her. However, I was hesitant to mention it; I'd learned that there are certain things you never talk about, no matter how seemingly obvious they might be. Yet, I was willing to take a chance, although another part of me argued otherwise. Her problem was

135

creating tremendous future health risks; she weighed over 450 pounds, and the extra 300 pounds was crushing her body.

I said, "At this point, I really don't have much to offer. We can try a different pain medication, something stronger."

She shook her head in dismay, becoming tearful again.

I took a deep breath and said, "I feel I really need to speak to you about the problem that's causing your pain because someday soon it will affect your other knee, hips and spine. You really have to lose weight, perhaps even consider gastric bypass surgery." I fell silent and waited for her response.

Lightning struck. Her hands suddenly released her knee. Her right arm flew up, and its hand transformed into a finger gun pointing directly at me, its index finger aimed at my head, its thumb cocked back ready for the trigger to be pulled, to fire words that would penetrate deeply. Her mouth spitting venom, her eyes burning hatred, she snarled and fired at me, "Don't you dare talk to me about my weight! Don't you dare!"

She pursed her lips, clenched her jaws and shook her head from side to side. Anger energies were rising. Her body was poised, alert and tense, ready to react, to move from word-bullets to physical aggression. She shook her index finger at me forcefully and fired over and over, directing the energies of her angry words into me. Her body started to shake, her face turned redder, her eyes blinked rapidly, and she fired more words.

Momentarily shocked by this encounter, I stepped backwards, away from the intensity. I caught my breath, as heat ignited in my abdomen, preparing me for battle.

Instinctually reacting, I plotted a counterattack, my thoughts and words already firing from my mind to return and neutralize the energy held in her words. I would win. Medical authority was on my side. Perhaps it was time to call security. We had ways of dealing with patients who went over the edge. My armor grew stronger and stronger. No way would she penetrate my sense of who I was. Her bullets now bounced off me because "I was right."

Don't try it, I was signaling non-verbally, *don't try it, don't you dare.* She had a real problem. Her anger was intolerable and had to be stopped. She had an anger problem!

Shaking, she held up both hands, moving them in a strangling motion and launching more verbal missiles to penetrate my mind and poison my body.

She sputtered, "I have friends who weigh over five hundred pounds who have no problems with their knees. I want you to fix my knee, that's why I came. I didn't come to hear a lecture about my weight." Her teeth locked down as if they were biting through my neck.

She moved her tense and quivering body to the edge of the exam table, ready to lunge at me, waiting for my slightest body shift to signal to her to instantly unleash all of her anger and frustration on me—The Problem!

Automatically reacting, my body was tight, armored and ready, my emotions were bunched tight and strong, ready to meet hers. My energy field of anger and power equal to hers. Visions of a physical battle began to unfold. I saw how I would react, take her down quickly and win this power struggle.

Then something unexpected happened. Maybe my warrior-self just wasn't up for another battle, for it hesitated. As if distracted, I stood there, catching my breath, waiting for a moment, as I felt a shift occurring.

There, in the midst of battle, my breath softened and my body relaxed as my awareness was drawn again to my heart center. Silently and steadily, the same process seemed to be happening to her. Her eyes moved slightly away from the intensely locked laser gaze she had aimed at the center of my head only moments before, and then they slowly drifted away and downward.

Self-reflection came. I realized I could be just as angry and violent as this woman was. Yes, there was a part of me that could be very angry and violent about what was happening in the world. Angry about someone else who "should" be blamed! Someone else! I could point the finger just as well as she, at *her* head. But, as I was once told, when one finger points at a problem, three point back to the solution. My judgment of the woman began to wane, and my heart opened more and more to her and simultaneously to myself. My hand-*gun* was beginning a transformation to a hand-*healer*.

I was reminded again that all anger and its frustrations come from our mental inability to control our lives and our inability to release our outer reality and break through. We get angry because we're unable to fix what we see outside ourselves, what we think of as wrong. We get angry because we can't release our addictive lives, and we must blame someone else. We're angry because we're unable to use our minds to get what we really, really want, even though we don't even understand what that is. Anger, therefore, is a defense against underlying helplessness. Anger helps us avoid the feelings of helplessness. And perhaps we were just not ready to engage helplessness, to move through and beyond it.

I knew not to challenge her when I walked in; to open up the vulnerable self inside her, to open up the feelings that weren't ready to be expressed yet. Why did I have to learn it again? How many times would I have to learn the same lesson?

I'd entered into her suffering and addiction, sacred things you just don't talk about. Her addiction was her friend; her attachment to needing food alleviated her aloneness and the separation she felt. It wasn't my place to enter. It wasn't appropriate for me to try to change any of her outer attachments and beliefs; they, too, were sacred, and they served her, they were a part of her identity. She needed to hold that together, it was her way of being and operating in life.

I'd encountered the fierce guardian of her deeper suffering and the doorway to the rooms of her despair. That door had kept me out, and appropriately so, for she alone could enter that space, if she would, in her own time.

Now quietness lingered in the aftermath of the battle.

I said, "I'm sorry you're having so much pain. Let's get back to trying another medication I think will help you some, and I'll get you an appointment with an orthopedist. The nurse will help arrange your appointment and return soon with your paper work." I said nothing more about our earlier intensities. It was time to move on; we both were exhausted by that war that couldn't be won.

I understood once again: Treat the symptoms. The patient wanted her pain acknowledged, she wanted me to treat what could be treated. I hadn't done that. The hunger, the addiction and the underlying suffering couldn't be dealt with; they were too personal, and she needed them. We all need our suffering: it's personal, private, untouchable and incurable. We hide the suffering under our everyday personas and awareness for a reason! It can't be dealt with, unless, as with Diane, there's a readiness. I told myself to stick to dealing with symptoms, not try to take people's addictions away from them.

Wisdom came again, reminding me of my own addiction, of the writing that had once consumed me. The angry woman had reflected back to me the truth I'd projected on to her, a truth I was not able to see or admit to—the truth of my own hunger, and yearning and attachments. The angry woman pointing a finger at my head also reminded me of the source of my own continued "problem": thinking, thinking, thinking.

Then I remembered Einstein's comment, "The problems created by thinking can't be resolved by thinking."

Yes, perhaps my stuffed head was just as heavy and burdensome and debilitating as her body was to her. My hunger for wholeness no different than hers, and just as misplaced, as a hunger for information, that was absolutely no different than hers for food, or the hunger others had for material things, money or intensity. Mental obesity, physical obesity, material obesity, financial obesity or emotional obesity were the new diagnoses, which caused a further explosion in symptoms needing care. These obesities seemed different; but all were caused, I sensed, by the same hunger, all were caused by the same yearning for something that seemed so far away and so un-accessible, that it might as well be labeled other worldly.

I began to see work differently during the coming days: looking around the department as everyone's work was consumed with staring at computer screens. In that moment there was no human interaction, just minds and their machines. As I returned to our shared physician's office, a windowless eight-by-ten-foot room, I walked past my colleague, whose small twelve-inch TV set above his computer was turned to CNN. It was announcing the latest news from around the world. Though I only occasionally glanced at it, the background noise and images of political conflicts, power struggles and wars now revealed additional crises to worry about. Man-made ecological disasters were now a habitual part of our landscape—a totally accepted self-destructive behavior of our planet.

What would it take for us to wake up and move beyond these crises to healing them? I sat in my four-by-four-foot cubicle with the 21" computer monitor in front of me and stacks of medical books above me, including the PDR, a 3,000-page book that described all the drugs available for curing or reducing symptoms. Directly behind me were two 21" monitors that instantly connected me to the X-rays, CAT scans, MRIs and ultrasounds of patients as soon as they were done, as well as all those stored from years prior. Next to these two monitors was a stack of three laptop computers, all connected to the main computer, allowing me, if I desired, to take the laptops into the rooms and do data entry while talking with the patient. We had to work faster and faster. More and more people were coming, with more and more symptoms and more and more drug needs to be managed.

When I began data entry into my computer terminal, it would take at least ten minutes to enter the patient's chief complaint, history, review of past problems, the physical findings, the diagnosis and plans. Then there was more time required to review and enter lab and X-ray studies and determine the prescription and follow-up plan. We doctors were doing our best, working as fast as we could. Though we didn't have golden arches with thick juicy burgers and greasy French fries to sell, our business was booming, and we were rushing because we needed to become the most successful McER.

Yes, electronic medical records were a boon, making us faster and faster, and our responses smarter and smarter, keeping us up with the increasing demand. We could connect to the world's best medical minds via articles and information on the Internet. We began using protocols to treat every patient the same. We had over 30 protocols, and many more were to come. This was good, fast, uniform treatment, and the "rules" insisted on it. The feedback and input from patient questionnaires put us into competition with other ERs and with each other. Who was the fastest and the best? The computers generated monthly graphs, statistics and numbers, along with personal "report cards." Technology and the corporate business model had come full force into the world of medicine.

Now, almost sixty years old, I was getting a monthly report card, upon which I was judged. Did I make the patient happy? Some physicians did not do so well, they needed "therapy" to understand the corporate model and defined way to treat patients to get them back to "normal." This was becoming pervasive in all institutions, being ruled from the upper levels of the tower above, someone powerful, giving others the capacity to judge and grade people. All totally unaware and totally unable to address the silent suffering of everyone in the control room of the tower or in its foundation—of separation from the heart. The bottom line—that was what was most important now. Other parameters that could not be understood, measured and reported such as healing and love were thus considered irrelevant.

How long could the Toyota business model for building cars, also work for human lives? Would the military mind set that was used for six thousand years of wars also work for the energetic hunger so many were experiencing now? Needing by design to completely ignore the needs of the body and feelings, with absence of the heart and love? Was the corporate model to be blamed? Or was it just more finger pointing by all of us, who didn't see the three fingers pointing back.

Onward with more gastric by-passes, more heart by-passes and more brain by-passes and more drugs needed, the bottom line improving every day even as the heart's presence decreases.

Fierce guardians, like storm troopers, everywhere, protecting old ways, even becoming ruthless to the cause of there being mental and physical answers only, precluding new ways.

The newest addiction to screens created a new challenge of virtual realities that manipulate us and make us more and more zombie like.

16

Light in the Dark

In the midst of darkness, of its loss we ask,
"Where is the light to be found now?"

What happens when we stare at the screens of a virtual reality hour after hour in the darkness, zoning out as the separation and disconnection from our hearts increases…

***

A six-year-old child came into the ER with strange symptoms. He felt ill and tired, and couldn't use his hands, they were cramped like partially opened fists that can't be opened any further. At first I wondered about a rare neurologic condition and did a neurologic exam that was negative in all other respects, then puzzled, I asked, "Does he play video games?"

"Well, yes, he did play a game all day yesterday, but we took it away from him last night, before he went to bed," the father replied.

The boy was quiet and looked down at his cramped hands.

"Well, if we have no further information, we'll have to do more blood tests," I said, knowing that comment might get us some more information.

"Do you have anything else to say before we start the tests?" I said, offering him another chance.

"I guess I do," he said, and then hesitated, "I started playing again when my dad left the room."

"So when did you stop?" I then asked.

"Well, I stopped this morning when I started to get sick," he sheepishly replied.

"Now we know why. Twenty-two hours of non-stop video gaming," I said, as I shook my head and turned to the father.

Like father, like son, I wondered?

Both living in separate rooms—staring outwardly at the surface of separate screens.

Minds lost in a new addiction to unnatural intensity—of virtual games of endless battles.

Men only capable of coming together for sports games and war games both real and virtual?

Bodies forgotten.

The addictive force of the outer surface light was very powerful.

What are our children being taught?

What do our children need from us now?

Is the inner light (focus) of love fading and nearly dead?

Our surface armor thickens as it must. We resign ourselves to sitting in the darkness in front of our computers again, looking outwardly at the surface light, as the daily battles continue, and we once again announce we are still in mental control of our two-dimensional, bipolar surface reality and doing fine. We don't yet know of another way to be with life—we only know the old way.

That night while driving home and listening to the oldies channel, the Beatles announce, "All you need is love". For a moment I feel the warmth inside my chest, just under my surface armor, it's just a small dose of heart, but it reminds me of the birth of another way, a new way. It's enough to go on for a while. But the intensities of separation continue and that birth is forgotten…

***

A young man came in deeply depressed. Over 600 pounds, he was unable to find work and had become completely disabled. The TV screen was his only life; he spent nearly eighty hours a week looking outwardly at the surface of a screen. When I looked in his eyes, I saw only the emptiness. I wondered again, as with others, how long was it since he'd been touched by a human in a caring way? One year? Five? Ten? Yes, probably ten, maybe by his mother? A modern-day zombie so empty on the inside? Living in a virtual reality with a virtual family. So many now living with virtual families; family members that never touch, never embrace, and leave us so hungry. A society of untouchables, unable to touch or be touched, stuck in a virtual surface reality that ironically still serves in some way to keep his life together.

My body says, "feel", my mind says, "no".

Our armor thickens over our hearts and the disconnection from its energies increases. Judgment comes, and then another layer of anger and sadness about the suffering of the body is added on the inside over the heart as it must. Resigned again to sitting inside the walls of our cubicles, being cubicalized, in front of our computers again. Looking outwardly, in the old way, at the numbers and statistics and information of our surface reality to confirm our successfulness, our bodies forgotten. The corporate model precluding any other way of engaging in life.

The daily battles continue, and we once again announce we are in control of our two-dimensional surface limited reality and doing absolutely fine. Our virtual bank accounts full. Not knowing that our real heart accounts were critically low, bankruptcy imminent. It was not time yet to change, as the old way was still needed and intact. The suffering of a corporate way of engaging life continued. We looked outwardly for more statistics to confirm our "winning game," not knowing that the breaking point and greatest loss was near. A loss that could be turned into the greatest win.

Some day later, while driving home in the dark, words of wisdom from the past come over the airways, from the oldies channel I listen to for healing. "What the world needs now"... It's been heard billions of times now? Dionne Warwick, another troubadour of the heart's reality, sings on, revealing the answer... "Is love, sweet love." I sing along, and for a moment I feel the warmth inside my chest, under my surface identity. It was just a brief connection to my center, a realization that indeed the full liberation of love was the answer. It was enough to go on. However, the separation continues...

***

A woman came into the ER, because of stomach pain.

"It started last night," she said as her eyes averted my gaze,

The husband was nearby and was overly concerned about the pain. He was anxious and even a bit angry at his wife that he was there. I felt his anger toward me also. I saw the clenching jaw muscles of his mind.

I knew the diagnosis without any tests.

I found no bruises anywhere.

The abdomen was a clever place to hit.

In private, after a pelvic examination, I asked if she needed help to break free.

"Tried once, that was enough," she said. Her emotionless face telling me everything.

He came back in.

He grabbed her by the arm.

The separate identities of angry mental guard and fearful physical inmate continued.

The rose garden, once the central focus of their lives, and its unifying energy were now long gone.

That ground, bone dry, was now the center of their life.

Going back home now, to a dusty prison for two.

The old ways of men trying to feel potency through controlling women would continue.

A man so angry and blinded by old ways of engaging life that he would remain unable to recognize his own impotency of the heart. A woman so tired and blinded by the old ways of engaging life that she would remain unable to recognize her own impotency of the heart.

The labels of bully and bullied or victim and perpetrator wouldn't matter with both in a heartless prison for two.

No one would get satisfaction with such a relationship filled with separation energies. No one would ever know another way.

Powerless to change; one day just like the day before.

Their guiding light—a high definition screen filled with stories of endless power struggles and hunger games and talking heads all creating more separation energies while holding on to the old ways.

The apocalypse of heartless living would continue.

Anger and sadness, my initial mixed emotional response to something I couldn't change, was quickly stored on the inside of my armor, to remain unexpressed. No judgment, for we knew no other way, never taught another way. Then back to sitting in the dark in front of our computers again, in the tower of power as mental warriors, as the daily battles continued and we once again announced we are mentally in control and doing fine. Mentally focused on the screen, body forgotten as separation from the heart center continued.

Driving home through the dark I sang along as the oracles of the past spoke again. "You've lost that lovin' feelin," by the Righteous Brothers, troubadours that revealed the truth about the unifying energy that was most precious, once, a long time ago, yet lost as we returned our mentally focused outer reality and then our virtual reality to try to find it out there. It was a remembrance of the greatest of gifts

It was just a small dose of unifying energy, felt as warmth, returning to the inside of my chest. It was enough to go on.

***

Months later an anxious young woman came in with a newborn baby only a few days old. "He saw it being born and stayed for one day and left," she said and then burst out in tears.

Years of living in an abusive outer relationship, willing to put up with so much, she seeking outer mental approval and validation of her physical-ness, as the power struggle involving her pelvis and body continued. He only wanted outer physical validation of his mental-ness, as the power struggle involving his mind and body continued. It was an ancient story of women seeking mental validation from men, and men seeking physical validation from women. Both unconsciously disconnecting from the heart's reality, knowing no other way, the validations offered to each other increasingly heartless and shallow. Mind versus body polarization intensifying.

The result was mind trying to control body, and body trying to control mind. Unsatisfied cheerleaders and unsatisfied warriors. Unsatisfying heartless sex, and unsatisfying heartless talk. Limited by only two choices—the old choices of either the body is right or the mind is right. The outcome preordained when the third choice of the heart and its reality is increasingly missing.

He did not want condoms to interfere with his sexual experience.

She was not able to access birth control.

His response a judgment—that his life was now messed up by her.

Her response was an acceptance of blame—the punishment that she would take care of the baby on her own. Oh the need to feel acceptance, oh the need to feel validated, at any cost, from someone else. If not a boyfriend, then at least a baby can do that for a few months or a few years, until they can't be embraced anymore.

Twelve weeks until back to work.

Twelve stress-filled weeks, and then separation from her baby. What of that baby's capacity to bond later in life? Does the bottom line include these costs to humanity as a whole?

He returns to his primary relationship on a screen for daily virtual battles and all the heartless sex he needs to briefly feel his body and then return to the control room of his mind.

She returns to her screen and primary relationship of soap opera families to share in her struggles and feelings to remain in her body. Her tears in the night, not just hers, but tears for all of humanity at the loss of the heart's light.

Millions and millions of times, unplanned, unintended, unwanted, unaffordable pregnancies leaving a vast part of society in endless forgotten cycles of emotional, physical and mental poverty. It was the hunger games of life for many individuals whose desperation would result in drug use to cope as prisoners or prison guards in a strange heartless prison and reality. No judgment, we didn't know another way, never taught another way. Just another part of the hunger games of the old ways of living in our end stage two-dimensional reality, of poor and rich, all so unknowingly hungry for the heart. No number of babies and no amount of wealth or power or Viagra ever enough.

I have no response regarding her fate or the expected fate of her child. I just don't have the energy to feel it, or the capacity to change it. I stay in my control room in my tower with its darkening walls of separation to such situations, continuing to believe in the corporate model of living and the superiority of the mind like the other men around me. In a place from where interpersonal relationships can be transacted via the screens that allow for keeping in touch mentally, but don't allow touch physically. Connected only to the internet of information, increasingly disconnected from the heart light, my body numb.

"So sorry," I said.

I called social services to see if they could help.

The virtual screens in the waiting rooms of life now reveal the end stages of our old ways of living in a two-dimensional reality with yet another gruesome murder of a woman by a man, and then a man by a man, and then men by men in progress. Suddenly the screen shifted to show two happy people on a beach. He just got Viagra. That happy, really? Are the happy people on the screen on antidepressants or antianxiety meds also? Then more happy people appear who just bought a pizza? Then more happy people drinking beer? Then more happy people who are buying a luxury car? All actors involved in a giant illusion. Going home to emptiness after brief moments of exaggerated happiness—things happening to go their way. The illusion that happiness is wholeness continues. The reality of the heart and wholeness still not understood or accessible, no stories of that, no ads for that.

The apocalyptic story of The Walking Dead returns, as we begin to identify with aging supermen and superwomen who are still alive and dealing with a new form of conflict. The greed and need created by heartless living leaving a desolate apocalyptic landscape. Once having lived successful, two-dimensional, outwardly focused, surface oriented and limited lives, they are now mentally stressed out and physically burned out; fighting a losing battle to not lose their hearts completely and become zombies that are zoned out and oh-so-empty.

Sitting in the darkness with virtual lights, life continued with the bang, bang, bang of physical violence and sex, and the blah, blah, blah of old talking heads we believe have the answers.

Totally absent in the darkness is the bloom, bloom, bloom of the heart—there is no channel for that. Head-on and hard-on only, no heart-on yet.

Our armor thickens silently on the inside with unexpressed and mostly unrealized and unexamined angst, despair and anger, as it must. Sitting in front of our computers, looking outwardly at the surface light again, as the daily battles continue. Still attached to the old way of engaging life, men once again announce our minds are in control of our separate, outwardly focused, surface limited reality and doing fine. Women still knowing the importance of feeling and nurturing and holding on to that role. The illusion that the old way is the right way continues. The disconnection from the heart for both continues to increase, resulting in more dis-orders and dis-eases that need tending to.

Some days later, while driving home through the dark, a song about a miner for a heart of gold begins. I sing along as a believer, with Neil Young, "keep me searching for a heart of gold..." Singing along, I am renewed by that petition and yearning as if I am mining for that heart of gold. In that moment, I feel the warmth of a golden heart within, and I can go on until the next day.

Many, many check in with us every day, "How's it going?"

We reply, "It's going fine."

Our armor is intact. Check.

Emotions controlled. Check.

Our mind and thinking in charge. Check.

Our body and feelings pushed aside. Check.

It is true; we are doing fine.

The old way of our two-dimensional reality and a self that is separate from others is intact and fully objectified and quantified.

Amount of unifying heart energy? Not on the check list.

We know no other way yet, beyond the old way and the un-manifested belief in the new way. We know no way other then looking at the bottom line. We know no other way, never been taught another way.

No judgment, full forgiveness in the time of healing to come. Then forgiveness transforming through grace to gratitude, because we didn't know any other way yet, never taught another way.

A time for every purpose under heaven, a time to kill and a time to heal.

Was it time yet for our increasingly intense, polarized and empty lives to go from a virtual statement of wealth and worth on a surface screen to becoming sacred and priceless again as a statement of the heart's worth in the book of life? Was it time to embrace the heart's light and its reality?

Relationship challenges were continuing to intensify with the rapid disconnection and divorce from the heart, both externally and internally. Old men trapped in the mental control rooms of the tower of power, desperately holding onto old visions of greatness and old mental power principles and disciplinarian roles that required suppression of feelings. Desperately displaying outer power to compensate for the unrealized inability and powerlessness and unfulfilled yearning to at long last come home their hearts.

Once caring women, the foundation that held up the tower for so many years, were increasingly unsatisfied with their old nurturing capacities and old roles being unappreciated and even denigrated, but were also holding on to them with desperation. Over inflated importance of the mind and deflated importance of the body. Over valued importance of the mind and undervalued importance of the body. Stressed out mind, burned out body zoned out heart. Absent heart, absent heart, absent heart.

The tower of power becoming dark in between the foundation and the control room; virtual lights telling us increasingly manipulated and manufactured virtual truths about what is happening and important. Watching only the "truth" that validates "our side's beliefs." Neither side's "truth" the great truth that would liberate us from a reality that is no longer enough. Though once hopelessly in love (hope liberated with the manifestation of the heart's reality) and on the ground level of life as heart-full equals, were we now separated in a tower as heartless angry wizards and angry witches? Were we living life with our mind and body separated and without a heart? Stern, desperate, scrooge-like men, nearly heartless and afraid of being overwhelmed by "deeply buried" feelings?

A silent and unrealized mantra creating men's life experiences:

The body must be controlled.
The body must be controlled.
The body must be controlled.
Deep feelings must be avoided.
Deep feelings must be avoided.
Deep feelings must be avoided.

Retreating to the mind, the heart's absence also increasing.
Anger increasing.
More hands becoming dark and Darth-Vader-like fists.
Life becoming darker.

Withdrawn women, nearly heartless, and afraid of "toxic" thinking?

A silent and unrealized mantra creating their women's life experiences:

The mind must be feared.
The mind must be feared.
The mind must be feared.
Toxic thinking must be avoided.
Toxic thinking must be avoided.
Toxic thinking must be avoided.

Retreating to the body, the heart's absence also increasing.
Anger increasing.
More hands becoming dry, withdrawing from nurturing.
Life becoming darker.

External power drives and external wealth is again confused with empowerment and liberation of the heart's full wealth. Humanity limited to superficial physical contact and mental communication, but no capacity for energetic connection from heart to heart.

How long must we silently suffer due to disconnection from our hearts? Staring at screens hour after hour, before men and women leave old roles and power struggles and polarized lives and claim new identities in the reality of the heart? When will women let go and ascend to the first floor and claim their own heart's power, and then unite with their newly enlightened minds? When will men let go of the increased toxicity in the highest floor and descend to the first floor and claim their own heart's power, and then unite with their newly enlivened bodies? Whole beings—hearts uniting minds and bodies within. The heart radiant, the mind enlightened, the body enlivened and sacred again.

When will we embrace new, empowering and powerful identities, and together step out of the first floor of the tower of power? Together exhaling the toxic dark air of separation still inside us, and then breathing in the unifying, life renewing air of love returned; to find the dusty and sterile surface of the earth becoming lush and green again with each step we take; centering and walking together into the sacred fields as healers and transformers of life. Our deep and expansive centered self and mutual loving, our mental self and mutual disciplining, and our physical self and mutual nurturing united for and moving into a new way of being-ness in a reality of wholeness.

My years of heart centering practices had kept me going and given me great insights and inspired challenging questions about our amazing journey home. It had served powerfully, but now I realized something else was needed. It was not enough to have a solitary practice of focusing inwardly through my armor and the emotional layers underneath. Focusing on that single light in the darkness was not enough to break free of our near total dependency on technology and its addicting and powerful light of information and its misuse. The virtual light had accelerated the loss of connection to the heart light. Indeed, it had seemed as if our generation was the one to be called on to make the great change and facilitate the shift that had been in the making for over 2,000 years, and yet...

I was stuck, stuck, stuck—waiting for the moment of great change—waiting for the break through. I was impatient, and yet, I was being taught to be patient, for the labor had its own natural timing. Months and months passed, and then suddenly, the fear of the death of an old self identity and the reality of energetic separation from the old self identity, and the yearning for the liberation of a new self identity and a new reality of energetic unity from within could wait no longer.

Yes, it had all seemed so complex and hopeless to my mind, with no power great enough to help us break free and pierce through the darkness and through our armor. Yet the solution, as I would energetically experience it, would be profoundly simple and beyond my mind's ordinary comprehension.

The reason we couldn't break free of our attachment to the surface reality of the mind and our nearly complete identification with it became very clear, as someone arrived who wanted to die.

Indeed, in the midst of our darkness, it would require one more death.

17
A Radiance of Love

*What is nearly impossible for one to do, and
extremely difficult for two to experience,
three or more can do easily.*

Knowing I wished to see such patients, the nurse said, "This chart's for you," and she handed me the clipboard.

She shook her head from side to side in dismay. "He said he's going to kill himself today, unless you have the answer." She gave me part of the patient's story—he was abandoned by his alcoholic father when he was two-and-a-half, he was addicted to drugs, he had attempted suicide multiple times, and had been in "treatment" many times, starting eleven years ago when he was only seven.

We both knew how little we had to offer such patients. Chances for meaningful change in someone who'd struggled this way for so long were very small. By this time, for him, turmoil was almost a way of being. His mind and old self knew no other way; struggling was the way he believed life to be. Death it seemed was the only way out.

I began walking toward room number six, intent on preparing him to go to the mental health crisis center. There they'd have the time and knowledge to stabilize him and get him back to "normal."

I knocked on the door lightly, and then opened it.

Jake was sitting with his legs over the side of the examination table, intently concentrating on the rhythmic up-and-down movement of his right forearm. His right index finger was slowly hitting and then pushing deeply into the cushion of the examination bed he was sitting on. Over and over he hit and pushed, as if a knife, releasing destructive angry into the bed.

He was tall and lean, much like me. His long, jet-black hair, dark brown eyes and skin tone immediately revealed his heritage as Native American. His clothes were all black—black shoes, black baggy pants, and a black t-shirt with the skull of an angry-looking demon, saliva dripping from its teeth, sprawled right over the center of his chest—right over his heart. A thick metal chain hung from the right side of his belt. Amateur tattoos, black only—some symbols and names, dots and lines, circles and triangles—were scattered on both arms. The residuals of scarring from childhood acne made him appear much older than his 18 years, and presently, his face was filled with frustration, despair and rage.

To the left in the room, quietly watching, sat his grandmother, who appeared to be in her early 80s. Her back was hunched over, and she was slight in build—no more than 4'10" in height. Around the middle of her slightly yellowed thick wool sweater was a thin band of small geometric symbols of different colors. Her shining white hair was obviously very long, judging from the size of the large bun on the back of her head.

I sat down on a stool across from Jake. His anger now intensifying, the rhythmic movement of his arm slowed down. He continued watching his index finger, pushing it down more and more slowly, harder and harder with each contact. Intermittently, he looked up and stared at me.

Defiantly, he said, "Give me one reason to stay." Then he resumed his hand motions.

I paused, searching for the answer. Then I began my usual response, "We have an excellent crisis center with people trained to help you. We can make arrangements for you to go over there now."

He looked up, furious. "You don't understand, do you? I'm done with all that shit. I want the fucking answer. Now!"

I insisted, "You need to go somewhere to get the right help..."

"You don't get it, do you?" he broke in. "I've been in and out of those places since I was seven. Those fucking doctors and nurses and fucking counselors don't know shit. I'm not going back there." He glared at me. "I want one reason why I should stay."

I remembered that Jake's father had abandoned him. Now I learned more and knew why he was at the breaking point. He recently smashed his car and was about to lose his job as a fry cook "because I came here today," he said accusingly. He'd lived 18 difficult years. It didn't seem fair someone that young—that anyone—should have endured such a difficult life and struggled so much. I kept searching my mind for the answer to his question. What was the one reason he should stay in this life—the one reason he shouldn't end it today?

It was obvious that returning to the crisis center wasn't for him, and yet he needed someone or something of depth to connect with. I thought, *He needs someone from his own cultural background, a spiritual leader or elder.*

Turning to his grandmother, I asked, "Is there an elder, a spiritual elder, for him to see and be guided by?"

"No." She shook her head and added, "There was one left, but he's been taken by the alcohol."

The male elders were gone, no men left, the old ways were gone, the old stories of healing from his tradition were gone; those possibilities were no longer available to him.

So I returned to the standard course of discussion. I stressed the importance of exercise to get out of depression. Physical movement alleviated depression better than drugs, I said. And discipline and goals were important—yes, a goal he was passionate about, something he could envision. He needed a goal he could direct his mental energies toward, something meaningful and fulfilling in his life that he could be successful at. "There *is* hope," I said. "If you can do these things, you can create a good life."

He kept staring deeply in to me, reinforcing the hollowness of what I was offering. None of it meant anything to him; he wanted only one reason why he shouldn't kill himself, one reason why he should stay in this life, and he wanted it now. This crisis had reached a critical point. There would be no tomorrow without the answer.

My mind went blank then. The need to fix ended. No real answer, just emptiness, nothing to hope for, nothing to stop the yearning and determination to die in someone who no longer feared death. The room fell silent, as did my blank, empty, surrendering mind.

Then grace descended, as it sometimes does when the stage is set and only despair remains, when hope for the future and fear of death are gone. Once again, a subtle warmth spontaneously began in the center of my chest. And then the answer came: his reason to stay.

I looked up to meet his eyes, and I said: "The one reason you don't want to kill yourself is because you've never experienced unconditional love."

"What?" he startled and answered.

"The one reason you don't want to kill yourself is because you've never experienced unconditional love."

He looked a bit stunned, confused, and then skeptical that there could indeed be a reason.

And I smiled; realizing at that instant that in some unique way what I'd just given was the answer, not just for him, but for both of us. But a second later the momentary satisfaction of having given the answer disappeared. As of yet he had no way to feel it or know it, to have it *happen* to him.

I paused, once again blank and empty.

Then, as if guided, I turned slowly to the left... and saw the fulfillment of the answer. Yes, Grandmother would be the key to our—his and my—healing in this time of crisis. Yes, with her, we could do it!

She was an elder, with the special capacities of the elder; no doubt she'd been holding a presence and love for her grandson's healing quietly and deeply the whole time. She had the capacity to give the love that would heal wounds on the inside that couldn't have been reached before that moment.

She was the key. It was her heart, her heartbeat, the ancient and healing heartbeat of a grandmother's heart that would bring us home. She could accept Jake exactly as he was, without needing to change him. She could ascend with the long forgotten gifts of love of the earth and sacredness of the body, to unite us with the heart. She could carry the long promised return of the heart, held in the stories of the ancient healers of her culture.

Ascending from body to heart.

I sensed that this was the first time in Jake's life when he was ready to receive this kind of love from two others, and in doing so, ready to give it back. With him, Grandmother and myself, we were all ready.

Three were ready to give and receive such love, ready to surrender at the same time. Three—A critical mass!

No beliefs held me back now. I had no doubt or hesitation as to what would happen next. Surrender to the process was absolute.

I explained the process of heart centering to Grandmother and Jake. Our healing energies would emerge from the place where we'd felt the deepest and most expansive form of love in our lives. At one time or other, even if only momentarily, we all have been graced with such an experience. We would ask for that experience to be known again, to tune in to the heart center's energies and then go deeper into that experience than we'd ever been before.

First, we stopped trying to mentally solve the "problem" with same old same old patterns of behavior and reaction to outer situations. Pausing our minds by becoming aware of our body and breath. I gave directions to relax the breath, and release bound tension in the body. Letting tension go on the out breath, and going deeper and deeper into the experience of calm. Softening the belly, relaxing the shoulders, jaw and forehead muscle. Breathing to release toxic emotions and lessen armoring or resistance to change.

"Feel the inside of yourself as you breathe," I said. "Feel the sense of inside becoming one breath, all of us from head to toe, one breath."

The third part of the sequence was to center, to connect to the energy of unity (unconditional love) available only from the energetic center in the chest, called the heart center. "It comes from right here," I said, as both my hands came toward each other, fingertips from the right and fingertips from the left, all touching the center of my chest. "We'll focus inwardly together on the light within. Just imagine it to be so, and it will be," I said.

The fourth part of the sequence was new, birthed because this was a time of great need, birthed because we were ready for the revelation and expansion of our healing/unifying capacities. This fourth part required something highly unusual that broke all the rules of normal encounters between doctor and patient and all the perceptions of what healing was and how it should look. It released all of the fear of touching and being touched, of healing and being healed so deeply, that nothing would ever be the same again. We prepared to release the outer garments of identity, of who and what we thought we were. We prepared to center, unify and shift for a time to embody wholeness.

"Grandmother," I said, turning to her, "We will be embracing Jake between us and infusing him with love. Please stand here, near the center of the room, and embrace your grandson."

"Together, we'll breathe with your grandson. We'll place our awareness in our heart centers and send him love and healing energy from the deepest parts of our hearts, as he sends it to us also."

Communion beginning.
Grandmother arising.
Wisdom arising.
Arising with all of its patience.
Arising with all of its dignity.
Arising with all of its love.
Arising from mystery, returning to heal...

Grandmother took a few slow steps toward the center of the room, raised her head up toward her grandson, and lifted her arms several feet from her sides, palms facing her grandson, expanding outward. She waited. He stepped forward, extending his arms toward the embrace of Grandmother's heart.

Heart to heart communion beginning.

Grandmother enfolded him, synchronizing her breath with his, as I'd explained. Then I moved behind him, heart center now warm, my left hand moving to then gently rest on his left shoulder.

The hand of the heart, touching lightly with powerful gentleness and full awareness... opening the entire body energetically, a place and a moment and an act where hope and belief are transformed into reality.

Arising from mystery, returning to heal...

My breath and my body relaxed into the touch, opening in receptivity to the infusion of unifying love that began to radiate both ways. Descending from my mind, surrendering my outer vision, returning to the heart to heal.

Descending from mind to heart.

Again shifting deeper into the process, we all relaxed our bodies, shoulders softening and dropping more.

Then my right hand was drawn slowly toward the center of his back, gently touching and bringing my whole hand to lightly rest over his energetic heart center. I felt that hand become warm, its energy moving inward to connect to Jake's energetic heart center, just as his heart center connected with me through the hand. My heart was suddenly awake, fully awake. My hands waited for the deeper invitation, the natural infusions of energy beginning, the opening enlarging, my awareness deepening its connection to his breath. Then when I knew the time was right, I slowly moved the rest of my body so that the front of my heart center was gently pressing against the back of his. Grandmother's hands moved downward, to rest between Jake's lower back and my upper abdomen, allowing a singular and intimate contact of heart to heart from behind.

Jake's soft and relaxed breath became my breath, became *our* breath. My hands and arms reached to gently touch behind and slightly below Grandmother's shoulders. Now we were fully surrounding Jake; our new eyes opened to see and sense inwardly, dying to the outer surface of what had been, stepping into the darkness. The pulsations of unity connected us as we journeyed inwardly, breaking free, breaking in.

Arising from mystery, returning to heal...

"Check in with the body," I said softly, to myself as well as to them. "Release any tension in the shoulders, jaw and forehead. Now we'll synchronize our full bodies' breath with Jake's and focus our awareness on the center of our chests, in our heart centers." It was the breath of the heart.

Now I could sense the light and energies coming from our entire bodies, one light and one radiance filling the emptiness and darkness. Vibrations of harmony and oneness were released, not only for the three of us, but on some level, its existence was felt and known everywhere.

The room remained quiet, filling with the supportive energy of unity, allowing the embrace to continue deepening. Our hearts' energies had fused our mind and body, three centers becoming one, as if orchestrated by unseen wisdom. Each breath filled the entire body with more light. I was aware of Jake's full breath and Grandmother's full breath and my full breath in synchronicity: three separate breaths fusing, becoming one, till we *were* one...

I experienced our bodies without form, transparent to each other's light, every cell emanating light in silent harmony, one mass of light, vibrating with oneness, creating a deep future remembrance of who we are: One breath, hearts united with bodies and minds, three integrated beings united in radiance, one radiance of being.

Arising from mystery, returning to heal...

A natural sense of completion came now; the deepest and most expansive expression of love had been touched and expansively shared. I released my position and then moved to

Jake's left side, keeping my right hand over the back of Jake's heart and my left over the back of Grandmother's heart as we continued to breathe together. Our three heads bowed toward something between us, created, emanating... the energetic field of the heart (Center).

Though the total experience seemed timeless, just thirty "real time" minutes passed, and the second half of the process, like the first half, ended naturally on its own accord.

Mystery now embodied and revealed.

Nourished to the deepest level, we had no more to do. Grandmother returned to her chair, Jake to the exam cart, me to my stool. We sat in a long silence, shifting slowly back to ordinary life and reality. The lightness of the heart and joy, however, continued to permeate throughout the room, emanating from all three of us. In the beauty of an experience that can be given no voice, we rested silently, fully immersed in its grace, all three smiling softly in the energetic mist of the heart's return that was released breath after breath, all three independently in love with life at the same time.

Indeed, through focusing inwardly, the great future love, the energetic return of the heart of wholeness, yearned for and hoped for, for so long, had occurred.

The voice of my heart, deep and centered, eventually broke the silence. "Jake, I would like you to go to your Grandmother's house every day for one of these hugs. Hug for five minutes each day." I explained to Grandmother the importance of her hand positions on Jake's back, with one hand over the back of his energetic heart center, and the importance of not moving the hands, and maintaining silence and full awareness and concentration on the breath and even feeling the warmth and beat of her heart. She would then remember the power emanating from the heart and then the body, as had taken place during our sharing in this room. She could bring that same memory and power into her sessions with Jake.

I said, "Centering on your heart center is a lot like turning on a light bulb—it radiates light in all directions, like a sphere. It's also like tuning into a specific radio station; it is always available, but we don't know that until we turn on the radio. When we place awareness on the heart center, we tune in to its unique location and unique energy: a state and frequency of balance and harmony that unifies us on the inside and makes us whole. We all have fallen in love at some time in life and can remember the ache of unity in our physical hearts because of our 'tuned in and turned on heart center.' It's very real and powerful the first time we feel it. We thought someone else was responsible, but the ache, what happened, was really inside of us. Later in life, like now, when we're choosing to awaken it again, it's subtler; it shares naturally with more people than just one. In fact, we can't help but share it, because it makes us feel whole to do it."

I smiled, "Great stuff, isn't it? And, Jake, when you hug your grandmother, remember and share the love you felt today. You infuse your grandmother with love, too; that's the way it works, two centered beings, filling up with the energy of the heart and then when full, letting it radiate out and sharing the energy."

Then I said, "I'm going to complete some discharge papers and arrange for follow up. We have to do this," I explained, "In order to follow what is considered the usual protocol and traditional way of dealing with situations like this."

Stepping out of the room, I continued to feel the wholeness within that had been created in that room. Body light and free, mind filled with gratitude; all filled and overflowing; all freed, freed by a radiance of wholeness...

Stopping for a moment in the middle of the ER hallway, being alone.

Softness of my breath coming into my awareness again.

Stepping to the right, resting my shoulders and body against the wall.

Body feeling soft and free.

Chest filled with warmth.

Mind bathed in radiance, face softening, faint outer smile appearing.
Grace with the in-breath; gratitude with the out-breath.
Grace infusing, gratitude pouring out as love—for life, for the body, for the mind and for the heart.
The fruit of the Eternal Garden of Life so sweet.
Exquisite.

The body and mind were now sacred, loved equally and fully through the silent energies of unity. And then once again the words came: *This will sustain me for months.*

It was a dose of shared heart energy far beyond anything I had ever experienced before. It was deep, expansive and life transforming.

Our awareness had penetrated through the layers beneath our armor, through self-criticism, self-denial, self-destruction, self-betrayal, anger and fear to touch the very center.

Touching the very center together, we experienced a death after all—a death of fear of love—fear of touching and embracing life in its deepest and most expansive form. Hearts were then filled to capacity, then overflowing, sharing. This death of old ways was really the revelation of an awakening and birth—of energy and how it works, flowing freely and intimately, from heart to heart.

After reflection, I typed up instructions for Jake's **stabilization**: for regular follow-up with a counselor **(information/talk based therapy)**, and also wrote a prescription for an antidepressant **(chemical based therapy)**, as I was expected to do. Then, smiling to myself, I wrote a modern prescription for life changing energy **(energy based therapy). It was a modern energy prescription for doses and doses of unifying heart energy.**

It said Rx: Heart Centering, and below it were the four simple steps: of pausing, breathing, centering and sharing.

P was for pausing—pausing old mental programs to awaken deeper mental capacities, to become "enlightened."

B was for breathing—breathing to release bound energy and thoroughly relaxing the body to become "embodied."

C was for centering—connecting our awareness to the heart center to become "empowered"—and starting the energy flow from the center of internal unity.

S was for sharing—powerfully and expansively **sharing** unifying energy center to center.

Our community of "three" allowed it to happen. *The key was coming together and simultaneously changing our focus of awareness onto our own center and simultaneously the center in the other*, and in doing so, changing the "energy field" in the room, knowing we are transmitters of energy and also **focusing on the exact location** that energy would be transmitted to, flowing freely and effortlessly penetrating though our armor. All hearts filled—A heart mass!

Knowing heart centering and then sharing the power. **Sharing to the deepest level was the missing element I didn't understand before.** We are all destined to know *and* share! The sharing brought us into the actual energetic experience and reality of wholeness. Sharing through presence, touch and embrace that were heart-full and then created wholeness. Energy, energy, energy, unifying energy that was what we were all looking for!

Returning to the exam room, I found Jake sitting up straight, calm and grinning widely. As I began explaining the need for follow-up, it became obvious that he wasn't listening; he was just grinning and grinning, and shaking his head slightly, wanting me to look into his eyes, to share what he had experienced. I didn't realize he also had another very important question to ask me.

When I finished speaking and gave him the prescriptions, he stood up and with all seriousness he said, "My grandmother makes wonderful banana bread. When I go to her house, may I have some?"

I could tell of the sincerity of his request, his genuine desire not to screw up anything, and I could feel his deep love for his grandmother, and his need to take in that love for life, held symbolically in that bread. "Sure, that would be just fine," I replied, feeling his joy inside of me, which was now my joy, also.

"And one more thing," he added, still smiling.

"Yes?"

"May I give you a hug?"

"Sure," I replied, smiling in return.

Then, as Grandmother watched, he opened his arms widely and slowly walked over to me...

There in the field beyond right and wrong... black armor and white armor moving toward each other, black and white, embracing and disappearing.

Eyes closing to feel the firm embrace, strong arms embracing each other.

Then arms relaxing, bodies relaxing, both fully releasing into the moment.

Right cheek softly touching right cheek, the warmth and beauty of divine flesh.

Waves of breath moving past our ears.

A sacred wind, subtle and sublime, carrying songs of joy from future and past.

Hearts fusing in a symphony of unity, resting bodies and calm minds, fully immersed in the power of the moment.

All hunger filled with precious eternity, one breath, one body, one mind, one heart, one radiant light of wholeness.

Filled, release beginning.

Two integrated beings.

Grins spreading over our faces, and then a hearty, "Ah,"

And the grips of hands on arms, tightening briefly, then letting go, filled with joy between us.

I will remember the warmth and depth of his dark eyes.

Home—home at last.

Embracing and being embraced by A Radiance of Love.

Part II

Finding

The challenging journey home transforms us, from reacting to life physically and mentally, to engaging it energetically and heart-fully. Through centering individually and with others we can step through the door from our old reality and self to a renewed connection to the reality of the heart. We can experience the whole self (balancing the energies of unity and separation in perfect harmony, as symbolized by arms and hands opened to life). Others are waiting for us—to embrace the profound and subtle beauty of life over and over. Our once-armored hearts becoming power-full and light again, serving as a gateway to wholeness (heaven/mind and earth/body united as a radiant event). Our lives now seen and known to be a journey, not to be judged or fixed, but celebrated in its entirety.

18
The Return of the Heart

Surrounded by a radiance of love, there is no more searching.

The following year in the ER was marked by many more unexpected heart-filling moments as well as four more profound life-changing encounters during intense life and death crises. They came in the form of a CEO at the breaking point with intense anxiety and chest pain, a deeply depressed machinist, a struggling cocaine and alcohol addict whose life was "falling apart" and a woman whose heroin addiction had destroyed her life. In each case three were present in the room and the heart fusion process was used.

As with Jake and his grandmother these experiences were so profound and beautiful that it often brought me into private moments of joyful and gentle tears thereafter. It could be said that to witness and experience such transformative events with others, makes the heart sing and the soul weep for joy.

I realized after my last encounter that—it didn't matter who, how old or how young, so long as there was one other person in the room with us to share, we all innately "got it," and were opened not only to the transformative experiences of sharing, but even more. With these big doses of unifying heart energy we were enlightened, enriched, embodied, empowered, enlivened, enjoyed and then experienced the fourth stage of human development as experiences of the heart's reality of wholeness.

No extensive explanation or understanding of energy or of centering was required; we were moved inherently beyond all mental programming, behavior patterns and cultural beliefs about what healing and love is and what we are capable of sharing. The energies of unity flowed through and beyond any surface armor of separation, outer gender, race and class identities and beliefs and connected innately into the heart's deeper reality—uniting heart with mind and body internally and radiating it outwardly to our small group.

Through deep heart-centered listening, there was deep unburdening and then the self-revelation of their own heart center. *And then* we shared silent heart to heart communion and communication.

In the ER during the initial discovery phase of energetic sharing through fusion, the heart centered embrace would be as it was with Jake. At other times when introducing fusion to others outside of the ER, other positions were used. But the focal point was always the same—The Center!

Outside of the ER we would start from the side with the center individual holding his or her hands over their heart first as myself and the other individual gently and lightly placed one hand over their hands and the other on their back. Our hands were like electrical paddles, as if gently infusing the heart with doses of unifying energy, awakening us all to the heart and the life changing energy that had become dormant, asleep and forgotten.

In the immediate aftermath I always felt as deeply blessed and expansively changed, as did the others. Often those doing the fusions with me would step back with amazement afterwards and make comments like, "I felt something happen to me, but I can't describe it", or, "This is impossible, but I feel so different."

Others would stand in silence, graced and dumbfounded, looking around the room for something, as if what had happened could be seen with the mind's eye. When I returned to the room after discharge paperwork was done, I'd find once-deeply depressed individuals excitedly talking about new possibilities with their partner, family member or friend. Or I'd find highly anxious individuals calmed and grinning, shaking their heads, talking with amazement about their experience of centering and the moments of experiencing the reality of wholeness that followed.

The Return of the Heart Center as a Power Source

These doses of unifying energy were just as unexpected and miraculous as romantic love had once been for me. It reminded me over and over that my youthful experience of romantic love was a wonderful foretaste of the heart's unifying energy freed in the expanded form of radiance, and the potential for all of us to fall independently "into love" with our own lives. Who'd have thought it possible to embody and share a radiance of unifying energy with many?

Romantic love: a beautiful, yet confusing and unconscious **external experience of "unifying energy" shared with one person** that leaves us "half-heart" or "half-whole." A powerful and wonder-filled experience, yet ironically it simultaneously marks the beginning of the next stage of our continued and confusing outer search and yearning for something more (to fill the other half of the heart inside us). Whereas **radiant love,** or more correctly, the radiance of wholeness it leads to, is experienced through the conscious capacity to deeply fall into unconditional gratitude for one's own life. Radiant love allows us to be independently full-hearted and full-filled, and then share the overflow of energy with others who are open to it, an experience that leaves all involved new and whole from time to time. This is an awakening, an **internal experience of unity, between mind center and heart center and body center that can then be shared with anyone else** who is centered likewise.

It was an affirmation of our underlying sense that there was a deeper and more expanded way to be with life.

It was also an affirmation of the many stories, both ancient and modern, from many cultures that in dark times the heart/love would return for a third time, but in **a way and form that would not be understood until it was experienced.**

Yes, we were destined to die and awaken, and overcome our fear of unconditional love, through releasing old limitations placed on it. With complete vulnerability and release of attachment to an old self, the door to the new opens fully. Coming together, as a new type of family, beyond sharing information and playing virtual and real games to share doses of unifying energy and experience the radiance and the reality of wholeness.

Sharing Heart Centered Power

And now, through this process, each individual also had someone else in their lives who knew and understood the unifying effect of heart centering—someone who could listen deeply as needed especially in times of crisis and remind the other of the path of growth they were on and share unifying energy from time to time. This was an empowering unfolding of new meaning for all relationships—to be there mutually for each other's awakening, growth and maturity into deep and expansive heart centered unity while heart-fully celebrating our outer differences. Creating, supporting and nourishing heart centered lives as we travel on the yellow brick road of centering into the rainbow of our wholeness.

Life gifted me, again and again, as individuals involved returned to see me, or I simply met them months later, discovering that the big dose (infusion) of "unifying energy" they'd received was still having dramatic effects on their life-circumstances. They were still experiencing the effects of opened hearts, relieved of tension and depressions, experiencing new possibilities and passion for life, transforming relationships with others and their jobs, and on occasion, they were even completely freed of their addictions. An internal love affair can do that!

Coming Home to Our Hearts and Experiencing Wholeness

We surrendered to the heart and touched the very center of who we were and allowed unifying energies from there to infuse and energize us on the cellular level. The distant remembrance of the heart as our mothers and fathers or grandparents embraced us as infants, and that we experienced briefly during romantic love when our hearts were pressed so closely to another's, was now found inside us. *Coming home, awakening to the inner triad, uniting mind and body with heart within, hunger satisfied on the cellular level*, we were able to release old imprints of separation pains that could never be released otherwise. We were reprogramming on the cellular level, becoming heart-centered selves, saturated by the energies of unity and entering into the reality of wholeness.

And what of the need for periodic doses of "unifying energy" to infuse and energize this renewed centered self, to keep it alive inside ourselves and with others? For no garden can grow without life-giving water.

After the last experience of fusion in the ER, my energy work inside the hospital ER came to an end. **I realized the hospital was a place for curing and not heart-centered touch or fusion**. It was a place for occasionally "energizing ourselves" during short breaks for personal self-rejuvenation. It was also a place for using heart-centered presence for deep and expansive listening when the rare "call" to listen was felt, and especially so for those in energetic crisis. But heart-centered touch and fusion could be misused or over used or be turned into a mental program for "fixing others."

I realized our institutions were meant to provide a stable environment to successfully stabilize our outer/surface lives. They change very slowly and were never meant to help us heal or fulfill our lives.

Just like our relationships in their current form, corporations and institutions serve to maintain the stable structure, function and order of our outer mentally controlled life called status quo. They also remain necessary scapegoats and can handle it, but they can't change and so remain "stable forces" until we again recognize the three fingers pointing back to us. We, and we alone, as individuals, have the power to consciously balance our technology with our humanity. Through our individual awakening these daily battles with our work slowly come to an end.

This insight allowed me to come into gratitude for the corporations and institutes as they are and released me of the need to criticize them or to use more energy to try to change them or their goals of outer greatness/success.

It was time to enrich our selves beyond our institutions and those in charge who are also silently suffering and hungry. With centering a new structure, function and order of living from the heart can begin. Then the deeper and more expansive changes and fulfillment of our lives can occur. That can then be carried within us through our presence, through our voices and through our actions and that will secondarily bring change to our institutions.

Heart-centered touch and fusion were never meant for fixing but to acknowledge the inherent wholeness that seeks revelation in every life story. Advanced practices therefore, will only be sought out by those who feel called and who are ready to come together; to mutually actualize their yearning for deep and expansive change through experiential validation of such a possibility. Specifically, you can't know what love from another is until you embrace someone. So too, you can't know what self-love is until you embrace yourself and then others equally.

And so it was time to integrate healing and wholeness practices outside the hospital setting for those ready to explore the emerging world of "Energy Medicine." It evolved into a living laboratory and energetic community as I began gathering and exploring with a small group of up to twelve people who knew heart centering, each of us responding to the next call of the heart—the capacity to gather for renewal from time to time as a heart-centered community. One morning every month with a larger group and one evening every week with a smaller group of three, we'd **embody and celebrate the heart's return and unifying capacities,** transforming—so to speak—to the centered self, *the integrated self.*

For a few hours we'd all shift and become the new heart-centered selves—transformers of life, energy savvy and integrated beings able to celebrate awakened centers. Through group heart-centering practices using the PBCs we shifted awareness inwardly and began the slow and subtle release of emotional energies trapped within.

Beginning within ourselves and then with others, using our bodies and voices we powerfully and subtly released "the

175

energies of separation under our armor" outwardly (no longer needing to direct them toward anyone or waiting to have them spontaneous erupt in destructive ways).

With some of the "dark muck" under our armor released, through subtle conscious "active energy release," we could access our hearts with far greater ease. With the departed "anger/fear energy," the void within could then be consciously filled with the light of unity, through centering to become "heart full" and then sharing it for renewal and wholeness with others.

The anger energy of separation transformed to the unifying energy of a new ally. Taming and flying our dragon is a modern mythological version of this theme of change portrayed in some current movies. Meeting our own fears face to face with others and in our own mirrors can be very liberating and fun.

Heart Fusion in the Laboratory of Life

Our individual fulfillment to overflowing with heart energy was also shared through heart centered movement (body-fullness), harmonizing voice (mind-fullness), self-embrace (heart-fullness), as well as through triads (two hands on the back of every heart), and quadriads and larger groups known as clusters in order to experience infusions of unifying energy as never before (mutual shared wholeness). Consciously connecting center to center. Long heart-centered hugs/fusions were available to everyone! The wisdom of the mind, the power of the heart and the courage of reconnecting deeply to the body were all experienced in one gathering, as a celebration of life and the energetic actualization of the reality of wholeness.

Fulfilling Our Destiny with Doses of Heart

We were destined to become energy savvy and go beyond living limited to a two-dimensional surface reality.

Destined to go beyond believing that only one other person could love (unite with) us at the heart level.

Destined to go from warriors and cheerleaders to champions and transformers of the heart and wise elders of the soul.

Destined to go beyond co-dependency issues, power struggles and relationship conflicts and polarization.

Destined to go beyond addictions.

Destined to go beyond stressed out, burned out and zoned out living.

Destined to go beyond chemical, surgical and talk based therapies alone to also use "energy" based empowerment.

Destined to go beyond being half-hearted and empty hearted to experience whole-hearted, light heartedness from time to time.

Our Heart-Centered Choice

Turning on our hearts regularly and sharing doses of heart energy with others was key to breaking free.

Where we place our awareness and invest our energy, and what energy is transformed into (a human being radiating unconditional love, or stuck in the mind with fear, or anger, etc.), is now, for the first time, our choice. When connected to our heart center and aware of other's centers, we affect each other with the energies of unity—whether our hearts are physically pressed against each other or a world apart.

Become a Transmitter of Heart Energy

The internet uses its transmission towers and connects us almost instantly on an informational level with each other to nourish us mentally. But now we are all in the beginning of connecting to the heart-net, the foundation of the shared grid of the subtle yet power-full energies of unity that is growing in our awareness, because it is already available here and now, yet in its infancy of use. Its signal still faint, waiting for more users and more frequent use to intensify the signal.

Like being a light and sensing many lights around you all being nourished by the same electrical grid, it's the shared "juice/energy" and being "wired together" that lets it happen.

Subtle energy is like light. It is both a wave and a particle. Both a current that energizes over distances as it invisibly moves out and as a field of energy that forms around the source that transforms it into a way of being. You might say we become the particle, and the wave is what emanates from us, or conversely we become the particle because of the affect the waves of others have on us. We can be a particle emanating separation or unity energies or a melding of both as needed—separate on the outside to do our separate outer work, yet anchored into the sameness within.

Now take a moment, centering to awaken and feel the warmth and energy of your center, remember how real it is, remember how it worked over a distance, changed the "energy" around you and "the one you once loved so deeply." Now shifting inwardly to the inner grid of heart uniting mind and body, the inner grid of wholeness, three lights coming together as one. Shifting and fulfilling the yearning of becoming a whole self, radiant, and now sensing the yearning and emerging wholeness in others across this planet, some nearby and some far away.

Actually, we are all, always being nourished by subtle heart energy yet almost always unconscious of it. All are being nourished by the same "life force" that is now increasingly calling us and emerging to reveal our wholeness, even in the midst of so many confusing "labor symptoms."

Take a moment again, center to awaken and allow yourself to see it, feel it, and sense it: the web, the grid, the network as light and energy covering the globe. Sense and feel yourself as having rays of this energy touch you and go into your center. Sense your capacity to draw from it as you give to it simultaneously. The force of unity works that way; the subtle energies and force of unity and wholeness work that way. Feel and sense your heart center now, sense my heart center, the heart centers of others. Everyone has one!

Shift beneath and beyond the important surface of outer symbols, songs and stories, beyond the surface of outer life and reality and the reflected light off of these surfaces that create the outer reality we "see." Use "insight" and tune "into" your center, tune in together. Let the connection deepen with each breath to embody and actualize that potential. Surrender to the images and feelings that life is offering you now. Surrender to the experience of a heart-centered self and unifying energy and the experiences of wholeness it leads to. Surrender to these emerging energies. Feel how the grid of unity is growing in strength every time it is used. One center streaming energy to another and back, creating the group energy field that fosters the heart's reality and then the reality of wholeness.

Remember, the internet came into existence through the efforts of a small but critical mass of individuals who believed it possible to create a "universal brain" to transmit information as energy through the air that would be transformed into images the mind could understand. Advanced mind to mind communication. So too, the heartnet, the energy network and "universal heart" will be fueled by unity energy (Heart Power). It will rapidly become a reality when a critical mass of individuals begin to tap into and transmit and receive the "energies of unity from heart to heart," creating group energy fields of unity, from energy we have all felt and know exists!

Be Energy Savvy and Save Your Life

Understanding energy dynamics comes automatically as we practice heart centering. It comes automatically as an embodied experience/wisdom, and then our mind no longer needs to understand how it works. We are saved from our old attachments to how we believe life is supposed to operate. We are saved from old mental programs and beliefs and a two-dimensional reality that remains important for outer interactions, but can't help us break free; they can't serve that purpose. We are saved from endless projection and trying to change others. We are saved from the need to be "right" all the time. We are saved from an old life of endless cycles of anxiety, depression and needs for addictive substances and drugs, both licit and illicit. We are saved from being impotent leaders and followers who are living with mentally created fear and hope cycles. We go beyond popular relaxation techniques that allow us to release the separation energy of stored tension for a brief period, by using centering **to fill the resultant void with unifying energy! Not just releasing the stress-full energy of separation within, but releasing and replacing it with empowering, unifying energy from time to time.**

We've gone to schools to help us physically survive and be mentally successful in the outer world, to win on the battlefield of life, as we unconsciously engaged the energies of separation. But we've never learned how to engage life energetically, to know what love or healing really is. But now the school to fully liberate the unifying energy through heart centering is open and for the first time we can learn how to love, heal and live deeply and expansively. **Then we will realize there is nothing wrong with us, we were just living in a box that eventually became too small.**

Going from success and judgment that were needed to become a separate self, to wholeness and validation of our lives by consciously engaging the energies of unity to energize a unified and whole self.

Going from separation to unity.

Center, Center and Center again, and Fill the World with Doses and Doses of Unifying Energy

What an unburdening, what a relief, what a gift for others, our children and us! We simply surrender to the heart from time to time to be energized by it, living and breathing **the heart's invitation of new levels of unity, visions, purpose and meaning for life** through simply being fully present, here and now, for others and ourselves.

Now all believers, for the first time, can being activating and experiencing their belief in love in the here and now.

Coming Home to Our New (spiritual/energetic) Heart Centering
Family

Giving deep and expansive unifying energy and getting deep and
expansive unifying energy in return!

19
Heart Centering

Simple-Profound-Immediate

Heart Centering is the foundation of Energy Medicine. A simple
yet profound process for reconnecting to the heart and
awakening and nourishing a life of healing, health and
wholeness.

Always Destined to Reconnect to the Heart, Through Choice,
to
Touch the Center and Be Energetically Free.

The PBC's of Centering
for energetic healing, health and wholeness

PAUSE—old mental programs and focus inwardly.

BREATHE—to fully relax the body.

CENTER—to be fully energized by unifying heart energy from within.

Share—unifying energy, center to center for the experience of wholeness/soulfulness.

***

Here is a brief taste of the heart centering process used to consciously access unifying energy. First do this with your eyes open. As you read, go through the hand motions that will assist you in moving awareness from center to center, and then do it again with your eyes closed as indicated. Start with clenched fists to honor that part of your life then has been successful at creating and holding your surface identity together. Then open your hands fully as you...

PAUSE. Slowly close your eyes and gently touch the center of your forehead (the pause button) with the fingertips of your right hand. Shift from an outwardly focused mind and old patterns of behavior and reaction to going inwardly and directing the focus of your awareness to the center of your mind, awakening to deeper insight and enlightenment.

BREATHE. Then move the fingertips of your left hand to your lower abdomen (over the relax button) and let them gently rest there as your awareness moves inwardly to the center of your abdomen. Focus on your breath and the rise and fall of your abdomen beneath your hands, filling the abdomen first and then the chest. Continue being aware of the inside of the abdomen, the inside breath—each inhalation and exhalation. Notice your body relaxing more and more with each breath. Drop the shoulders and then release the jaw and forehead muscles with each breath. Use the "Ah" sound to actively and consciously release additional bound tension from the body and for as long needed. Releasing stress from within the body, this "breath" gives you the physical space to transform.

CENTER. Now gently and slowly, with awareness, bring your hands together over your heart center (the play button). Touching every so lightly, first with the right hand and then the left hand over it with thumb tips touching. As you move your awareness from your breath to your heart center within, allow an image of light to ignite in the center of your chest beneath your hands. Feel the power as you feel the warmth of this light heating your chest and hands. Sense the infusion of unifying energy expanding from your center as it fills you from within. Let that light and warmth and calm expand with each in-breath, filling your body with the unifying energy of the heart center. This "center" gives you the power to change.

SHARE and share the unifying energy of centering. Allow yourself to be the embodiment of your essence, beyond mind, body and heart—becoming a unified, whole self. Then, having been nourished and transformed, open your arms to your sides and complete the process, through sharing this heart-centered energy, and radiating it outwardly through your armor— energetically touching, nourishing, and subtly gifting the lives of those around you center to center to center.

Again, feel the grid of energy forming center to center. Sense into the current and the light, forming a web and grid of "unifying energy" in whatever way naturally comes to you.

Now again, surrender to the natural capacity to become aware of others who are open, as if around you, of their centers and yours. Rest into this image and feeling. Fill yourself from all directions from others as you fill others in return, becoming a light amongst lights. This is the conscious blueprint and beginning of the "energetic community of the heart." Now, with complete awareness and connection to your heart center continuing, open your eyes and see yourself and the world anew. The capacity to connect to life in such an expanded way with eyes open will be very brief and subtle at first and then increase with time.

With time, this foundational practice of centering by going through the main stages of the PBC's will begin to reveal its energetic nature more fully. It will become one flowing energetic event that involves, mind, body, heart and soul (expanded essence and sense of self) as you automatically pause and...

Just Center Yourself to start the energy flow from within **and share the energy** center to center with others and experience mutual wholeness.

Yes, just center and shift, and the whole-self state is instantly powered up, anytime and anywhere, even with your eyes open.

***

Next time when you are in front of a mirror **look at the surface reflection of who you are, the surface self.** Then take a few centered breaths and relax completely, as you look deeply into your own eyes. Deepen your gaze while remaining aware of your center, and imagine you are connected to the center of the one in the mirror. Continue to deepen until you recognize, you are looking at the man or the woman in the mirror that has made the change and is transformed here and now. Though the same on the outer surface, only this centered self, **the new-self, connected consciously to your own core, the deepest self,** can make that expansive change you've always yearned for. Then closing eyes, embrace yourself gently and feel it deeply. Center, give yourself a dose of heart, and let the unifying energy break free as your hands open to your sides.

***

Powering up your heart with various forms of centering practices, you will be able to consciously release your attachment to outer stress filled living from time to time. You will simply and increasingly become centered, conscious, connected and energized by the grid and matrix of unifying energy.

Over and over your center will begin to engage you spontaneously—after all, even though you're almost always unconscious of it, you are *here now* being infused with some heart energy, yet are unaware of it. It will increasingly call with more obvious spontaneous feelings of warmth in your chest. Sometimes it will awaken you with a dream and images that are "sent" from your unconscious realms to support your journey to wholeness. Sometimes it brings insight as you revise your old "concretized" judgments about reality and life. Sometimes the warmth is associated with someone in your outer life that spontaneously comes to your awareness, and then you grasp how energy flows unconsciously from one to another. Always supporting and nourishing both of you on the energetic level, but now it becomes conscious, empowering and liberating to share.

Our common capacity to engage the center's unifying energy and share it will be what carries us into our next stage of human development and the wholeness it holds for each of us. Beyond the mind's two-dimensional comprehension of life are energetic three-dimensional heart to heart relationships and networking, amplified by the close or distant proximity of other opened hearts/centers.

Others are waiting for you to share and celebrate the Heart's Return, just open the door and come home from time to time.

"Power Up with Daily Doses"
Our daily choice: Doing what we've always done and always getting what we've always got. Or centering and changing by consciously changing our state of consciousness and giving ourselves and others, daily doses of unifying, life fulfilling, radiant energy. From unconsciously identifying

with the reality of the mind or body to shifting and consciously identifying with the reality of the heart.

Of course the challenges will come over and over, but now the "Well of Life-Renewing and Life-Transforming energy" is available. Drinking from the center from time to time will bring us into a celebration of the beauty of life and our journey home to our heart, the joy can be that great!

Consciously engaging the centered way of being will **sustain and nourish us** and create the foundation of a heart centered and "whole" world for our children and others to come. What a living legacy is that!

The new calling: From our heart center, to live with full hearts.

The new external symbol: Light radiating from the center of a heart.

The new internalized symbol: Light radiating from inside, from our heart center.

The new focus: Our heart center.

The new way of interacting: Heart-centered and energetic.

The new power: Heart-centered "unifying" power.

The new dimension: 3D of the heart center

The new self: Heart-centered and whole.

The new heroes and heroines: Heart-centered champions, empowered from within.

The new presence: A heart-centered presence.

The new touch: Heart-centered touch.

The new embrace: Heart-centered embrace.

The new relationships: Heart-centered, heart filling and whole.

The new sexuality: Heart-centered and transforming.

The new passion: Heart-centered service to life.

The new wealth: Heart-centered wealth (a full heart).

The new power structure: Heart-centered and heart-powered.

The new community: Heart-centered community.

The new family: Heart-centered and deeply nourishing.

The new society: A heart-centered society.

The new network: The Heartnet.

The new gifts: Heart centering for The Wisdom, The Power (Love) and The Courage to Change (expand our reality).

This is new heart-centered vision for humanity, this is the new heart centered way of being, this is the new heart-centered process to usher in the next stages of human development. This is new gifting and empowering of others with the heart centering process to engage life energetically, for more and more spontaneous and unexpected experiences of enjoyment and wholeness within the reality of the heart.

20
The Heart's Five Attributes

Through heart centering over and over the heart's attributes are increasingly experienced as spontaneous gifts, beyond our ordinary mental understanding or capacity to manifest.

With centering we automatically begin engaging the reality of a full heart and naturally experience...

Unconditional Love as we embrace all of who and what we are with deep and abiding gratitude.

A Healing Presence that transforms our "wounds" of separation and brings unity and wholeness to our lives.

Innate Harmony felt as a deep indwelling calm, balance and peace, even as there are storms around us.

Compassion for ourselves and others and our prior power struggles on the road to wholeness, through realizing we had no understanding of how to find our hearts again, until now. How profound and beautiful this heartfelt attribute becomes when actualized.

Service to Life as felt in the new passion, meaning and purpose of life, to joyfully share modern energy principles and the heart centering process and the heart's power and spontaneous experiences of wholeness.

Just Center Yourself and Center with Others

21
The Gift of Centering

There are so many wonderful centering practices that ignite the enjoyment of life from time to time. They also ignite the dreams and insights and experiences that validate the importance of the inner spiritual (energetic) journey home to the heart and back out with the gifts of unity and wholeness to share with others.

Sharing a heart-centered presence with others and teaching the heart-centering process has been the most gratifying experience of my medical career. How a process so simple could be so profound in its effects on others and myself still surprises me. But the centering experience called love in the past of course was also reality shattering so why should this new form of love and healing and harmony and compassion be any different in its reality shattering and fulfilling potential.

And so this, I believe is our destiny: to become energy savvy and use centering to fill our hearts and embody the new passion, meaning and purpose of life, of sharing the energies and reality of unity and wholeness over distance and in person. It starts with consciously sharing with just one person in as little as thirty seconds, it then moves easily to groups of three and more creating heart centered communities through regular gatherings. Validating the power of love through loving ourselves so deeply and expansively that we can break free of our health crisis caused by the separation from our hearts and unifying energy so critical for our wellbeing. Becoming heart-centered selves that are transformers and then wise soulful elders.

Doses and doses of unifying energy to enter the energy pool we live in every day. Doses and doses of unifying energy that create the heart's reality of calm, balance, empowerment, embodiment, enlightenment, enrichment, enlivenment, enjoyment, integration and wholeness over and over again.

Centering Ourselves
To empower heart centered calm, integration and wholeness.

22
Life Fulfillment

Beyond the limitations of personal outer success the experience of energetic life fulfillment with others awaits us.

I hope the stories and insights in this book about our collective journey home through reconnecting to our hearts have touched you as deeply as living them touched me.

I invite you to become an integral part of a critical mass of million and millions of individuals, to become energy savvy and share the process and unifying energy of heart centering. Through using our social networks to share the process we can rapidly begin surrounding ourselves with others who know how to access their heart center and it unifying energies and reality.

Together we can create a worldwide movement of reconnecting to our hearts, for renewing, empowering and fulfilling lives through shifting into the reality of the heart and wholeness over and over again. Fulfilling our destiny to heal deeply and expansively from our center.

A final realization with our "Enlightenment" is that its energy, energy, energy, its all about energy that unifies us and makes us whole. What a glorious day to realize that its not something, or somewhere or somebody out there that we seek, but energy, energy, energy, unifying energy. Energy that is available to anyone, anywhere and at anytime.

At this time, there is no greater gift, no greater legacy, no greater call then to reconnect to our hearts and liberate its unifying energy for ourselves and all of humanity.

It's time to embrace and embrace Energy Medicine.

It's time to Rx: Heart Centering for doses and doses of unifying energy to energized a heart centered self and liberate our heart's full power.

Begin the vital first step to energetically fill your heart and experience its reality of healing, health and wholeness by…

-Understanding the Universal Law of Creating Realities.

-Learning Basic-Heart Centering practices.

-Using our technology to accelerate our spiritual/energetic growth.

-Gathering with others to renew and fulfill our lives.

-Becoming a teacher and co-facilitator of heart centering as a foundational and universal energetic process that fosters energetic healing, health and wholeness.

-Enriching yourself through our website and our programs for energizing heart centered lives.

-Recommending this book and the basic heart-centering practices to others through your social networks.

It begins with information shared from mind center to mind center, it becomes reality when energetically embodied *and* shared from heart center to heart center.

Fulfilling the Great Prayer and Petition for Unity.
Networking Heart to Heart, to reconnect to our hearts and liberate our heart's full power and create the Heartnet of Humanity for ourselves, for our children and their children and for our planet.

Appendix

Understanding Your Life as a Journey to Wholeness.
The Four Stages of Human Development.
This is a template of the three energy centers and four stages of human development. It includes some metaphors from nature and even characters from stories of the journey to wholeness. It is energy (the power, spirit, chi, prana, life force) that moves us along and energizes each stage. Here the first half of life is outwardly directed, while the beginning of the second half is inwardly directed. The conflict between the reality of the old ways and the new ways continues until we surrender from time to time to the Soulful/Whole self, experienced as the integrated, unified and shared fourth stage.

The First Half of Life		The Second Half of Life	
The Body	The Mind	The Heart	The Soul
Her-story	His-story	Our-story	All-stories
Goddess	God	Healer	Sage
Moon	Sun	Star	Cosmos
To Feel	To Think	To Love	To Be
Matter	Information	Energy	Essence
Unconscious	Programmed	Conscious	Cosmic
Dependency	Separation	Unification	Wholeness
Singularity	Duality	Three-ness	Oneness
1-D	2-D	3-D	4-D
No Self	Outer Self	Inner Self	Whole self
Survival	Success	Acceptance	Fulfillment
Nurture	Cure	Heal	Transform
Cheerleader	Warrior	Transformer	Mentor
Roots	Branches	Flower	Fruit/seed
Lion	Scarecrow	Tin man	Dorothy

G. Burgstede, 1994

Your Life Journey
↓
The First Stage (**body** oriented)
↓
The Second Stage (outwardly oriented **mind** separated from body)
↓
The Birth of the Third Stage (inwardly oriented **heart**)
↓
Conflict/ Transition between the second (**Mind/Body**) and third (**Heart**) stages
↓
Resolution of with the Emergence of the Whole/Soul Self (**Body-Heart-Mind** unified and integrated inwardly and outwardly through sharing).

First, energy flows to the body.
Second, energy flows to the mind.
Third, energy flows to the heart.
Fourth, energy flows freely to and from the whole self (soul-full).

First, we experience the physical energies of unity.
Second we experience the mentally created energies of separation.
Third we experience the heart-focused energies of unity within.
Fourth we experience the energies of unity and separation being in balance with each other, i.e. the experiences and images of wholeness.

Rx: A Dose of Heart

Body → Mind → Heart → Soul

Realities of Life
The one-dimensional reality of the body.
The two-dimension reality of the mind.
The three-dimensional reality of the heart.
The four-dimensional reality of the soul (our
essence or essential self).

The Transition Period

Mental Self		Transitional Self		Whole Self
Smart	→	Confused	→	Wise
Armored	→	Empty	→	Power-Full
Strong	→	Afraid	→	Courageous

Your story of the journey home to the heart of who and what you are becomes the greatest story ever told and the greatest journey ever taken. For through this journey, beyond your superman or superwoman self, you are gifted as a centered self with your capacity to renew your connect to your heart's rejuvenating energies and with others experience the reality of wholeness; a process that becomes **as simple as clicking your heels together.**

Center for the Power to Change.

In this moment, in this very moment,
your heart is calling you and inviting you to…
Just pause and feel the warmth in the center of your chest,
and see the light and sense the calm
and radiate it outwardly and receive it in return.

Algorithm of Life *and* Love

Embraced at birth

↓

Embracing another

↓

Silent suffering due to loss of heart connection

↓   ↘

Continued   Centering now

Suffering   Embracing ourselves and others now

Experiencing unifying radiance now

↓

The center revealing itself

just before death as we

embrace our life and others and

experience unifying radiance when dying

About the Author

Gil Burgstede, M.D, was born in Amsterdam, The Netherlands, and as a child immigrated with his parents to Southern Wisconsin. He is a graduate of the Medical College of Wisconsin and completed his residency through the University of Illinois. For the past 40 years he has practiced medicine, first as a family physician, then as an emergency room physician for nearly twenty years and lastly as an urgent care physician. In addition, he has had twenty five years of study in the realms of energy dynamics, energy healing, energy medicine, critical mass creation, the structure, function and order of realities and how they are maintained energetically, stages of human development, dream analysis, Jungian psychology, mythology, a personal understanding of the masculine journey from mind to heart to then experience wholeness, a secondary understanding of the feminine journey from body to heart to then experience wholeness, the ancient origins and stories of the world's religions and healing traditions and the modern energetic integration of "heart energy" into daily life. He has guided individuals and groups in accessing their centers for renewal and life transformation.

"It all comes down to the simple act of centering and sharing the heart's power (energy of unity) so we can experience what cannot be taught in any other way: to embody the energetic experience of wholeness."

Gil shares his passion for heart-full living with his life partner of forty years, Janis DeLuca, who guides women on their uniquely different path from body to heart to then experience their wholeness. They have two adult children, Adam and Annie.

A physician once said, "A life changing dose of the most powerful medicine in the world is needed."

A patient then asked, "Well how do we do that?"

The physician, now older and wiser, smiled and replied, "We center ourselves and embrace ourselves and others so frequently and powerfully that it changes us and our world."

www.ingramcontent.com/pod-product-compliance
Lightning Source LLC
Chambersburg PA
CBHW052000090426

42741CB00008B/1484